M6

The Critical Idiom

General Editor: JOHN D. JUMP

---

33 The Picaresque

In the same series

The Picaresque/

Harry Sieber

Methuen & Co Ltd

First published 1977
by Methuen & Co Ltd
11 New Fetter Lane London EC4P 4 EE
© 1977 Harry Sieber
Printed in Great Britain by
Fletcher & Son Ltd, Norwich
Bound by
Richard Clay (The Chaucer Press) Ltd.,
Bungay, Suffolk

ISBN 0 416 82710 1 Hardback
ISBN 0 416 82720 9 Paperback

Distributed in the USA by
HARPER & ROW PUBLISHERS INC
BARNES & NOBLE IMPORT DIVISION

Para Antonio Recio Gago,
pícaro de Córdoba y
camarero de don Bigote

Contents

General Editor's Preface

The volumes composing the Critical Idiom deal with a wide variety of key terms in our critical vocabulary. The purpose of the series differs from that served by the standard glossaries of literary terms. Many terms are adequately defined for the needs of students by the brief entries in these glossaries, and such terms do not call for attention in the present series. But there are other terms which cannot be made familiar by means of compact definitions. Students need to grow accustomed to them through simple and straightforward but reasonably full discussions. The main purpose of this series is to provide such discussions.

Many critics have borrowed methods and criteria from currently influential bodies of knowledge or belief that have developed without particular reference to literature. In our own century, some of them have drawn on art-history, psychology, or sociology. Others, strong in a comprehensive faith, have looked at literature and literary criticism from a Marxist or a Christian or some other sharply defined point of view. The result has been the importation into literary criticism of terms from the vocabularies of these sciences and creeds. Discussions of such bodies of knowledge and belief in their bearing upon literature and literary criticism form a natural extension of the initial aim of the Critical Idiom.

Because of their diversity of subject-matter, the studies in the series vary considerably in structure. But all authors have tried to give as full illustrative quotation as possible, to make reference whenever appropriate to more than one literature, and to write in such a way as to guide readers towards the short bibliographies in which they have made suggestions for further reading.

John D. Jump

University of Manchester

I

Prologue: some definitions

> Picaresque: 'Belonging or relating to rogues or knaves: applied esp. to a style of literary fiction dealing with the adventures of rogues, chiefly of Spanish origin.' *OED*

The word 'picaresque' seems to have shared the same fate as other literary, critical and descriptive terms such as conceit, irony, satire, naturalism, classicism and romanticism, in that attempts at precise definition have produced more confusion than understanding. The *Oxford English Dictionary*, while in no sense the ultimate authority, suggests three essential characteristics which help to locate a point of departure. First, the picaresque is a *literary* phenomenon, a work of fiction which is concerned with the habits and lives of rogues. Secondly, it is a *style* of fiction, that is, a kind or type of work which is distinguishable from other fictional styles. And third, its origins are found in Spain, implying that it has a 'history' whose genesis can be located in space and time.

Few definitions of the picaresque have improved on the brief description found in the *OED*. In 1895 Fonger de Haan (*An Outline History of the Novela Picaresca in Spain*, not published until 1903) defined picaresque fiction as 'the autobiography of a *pícaro*, a rogue, and in that form a satire upon the conditions and persons of the time that gives it birth' (p. 1). He makes two important additions to the *OED* account, seeing it as an autobiography and its 'style' as a 'form' of satire, an idea recently taken up and fully explored by Ronald Paulson in *The Fictions of Satire*, 1967. Soon after de Haan had defended his dissertation at Johns Hopkins, Frank Wadleigh Chandler presented his Ph.D. thesis at Columbia University. The first part, 'The Picaresque Novel in Spain', was published with the title, *Romances of Roguery: An Episode in the*

History of the Novel, 1899. Chandler's book on the picaresque novel is still viewed, particularly by non-Hispanists, as the best authority on the subject. His description of the rogue narrator, the *pícaro*, is now a commonplace in literary criticism of the picaresque:

> The picaresque novel of the Spaniards presents a rogue relating his adventures. He is born of poor and dishonest parents, who are not often troubled with gracing their union by a ceremony, nor particularly pleased at his advent. He comes up by hook or crook as he may. Either he enters the world with an innate love of the goods of others, or he is innocent and learns by hard raps that he must take care of himself or go to the wall. In either case the result is much the same; in order to live he must serve somebody, and the gains of service he finds himself obliged to augment with the gains of roguery. So he flits from one master to another, all of whom he outwits in his career, and describes to satirize in his narrative. Finally, having run through a variety of strange vicissitudes, measuring by his rule of roguery the vanity of human estates, he brings his story to a close. (pp. 45–6)

Chandler's characterization of the Spanish rogue is accurate for the most part, although it actually defines an 'ideal' type of rogue rather than any particular *pícaro*. This kind of generalization anticipates the attempt of Stuart Miller (*The Picaresque Novel*, 1967) to define an 'archetypal' picaresque novel in terms of its most salient features, leaving little room to consider the changing elements of the genre from country to country over an extended period of time. Chandler's definition, however general it may be, clearly distinguishes the picaresque novel from a larger body of fiction which he calls the 'literature of roguery'. The latter includes criminal biographies, beggar books, vocabularies of thieves' cant, conycatching pamphlets and jest books. Very simply put, the picaresque as a narrative genre, as distinct from these 'anatomies' of rogues, tricksters and beggars, has both a plot and a single narrator. The subject-matter is often shared by both traditions, but only in the picaresque novel is it shaped into an 'artistic' form and narrated from the viewpoint of the *pícaro*.

These conventional definitions of the picaresque are virtually forgotten by more recent critics who tend to stretch the term to include 'any novel in which the hero takes a journey whose course plunges him into all sorts, conditions and classes of men...' (Walter Allen, *The English Novel*, 1954, p. 18). Robert Alter (*Rogue's Progress*, 1964) virtually repeats earlier definitions whereas Claudio Guillén (*Literature as System*, 1971) distills the picaresque narrative to the 'confessions of a liar' (p. 92). A. A. Parker (*Literature and the Delinquent*, 1967) counters the confessional element, claiming that the autobiographical viewpoint 'is not essential; the distinguishing feature ... is the atmosphere of delinquency' (p. 6). And Ihab Hassan (*Radical Innocence*, 1961) goes so far as to deny even its Spanish origins by seeing it as an English phenomenon. Christine J. Whitbourn (ed., *Knaves and Swindlers*, 1974) goes to the other extreme by locating the roots of the picaresque in the fourteenth-century Spanish *Libro de buen amor* or the fifteenth-century Catalán work, *Lo spil, o libre de les dones*.

It is obvious that a great deal of confusion still exists both in locating the Spanish origins of the picaresque and in defining the extent to which the term is applicable to fiction outside Spain. My purpose will be to clarify these issues by approaching the picaresque in its strict sense as a literary genre and then by following its itinerary outside Spain via 'translations' and 'imitations' of specific novels. I will thus spend a good deal of space outlining and describing themes and plots in order to obtain a cluster of 'picaresque conventions'. I will also stay close to the history of the genre by weighting my discussions with dates and places of publication in order to sketch a profile of the picaresque tradition. I will then attempt to define a 'picaresque myth', that is, a story, plot, or 'situation' which can be seen working in certain nineteenth- and twentieth-century works. Here my assumption is that reading them in a specific 'mythic' tradition will add to their appreciation and understanding within the wider contexts of fiction. My intention is constructive. If revitalized and properly understood, the term 'picaresque' can still be of some use as a literary-critical category in the general domain of the critical idiom. Finally, an anonymous seventeenth-century reader referred to one Spanish picaresque novel as being a mixture of 'burlas y veras' ('jests and truths'), pointing out perhaps the genre's internal uneasy blend of humour and seriousness. My interpretation will emphasize the latter at the expense of the former.

2

The picaresque in Spain: origins and definition

The English word 'picaresque' is borrowed from the Spanish *picaresco* (Mateo Alemán, 1599) or from *picaresca* (Alfonso de Pimentel, *c.* 1587). These first attestations in Spain are adjectival forms of the noun *pícaro*, usually translated into English as 'rogue, knave, sharper,' into French as 'gueux, voleur' ('beggar, thief'), into German as 'Schelm, Abenteurer' ('rogue, adventurer') and into Italian as 'pitocco, furbone' ('vagrant, rogue'). Unfortunately, *pícaro* is a word whose etymology is uncertain and whose semantic history is complex. Joan Corominas, having reviewed several theories, concludes that it comes from some form of the verb *picar* ('to prick, puncture; nibble, bite') which at some point came into contact with thieves' cant (*germanía*) to give it the general meaning we ascribe to it today. From there it made its way into the public linguistic domain. When the word first appeared (1525) in the expression 'pícaro de cozina' ('scullion'), however, it seemed to have nothing to do with the notion of delinquency or immorality. The *pícaro* was involved in menial jobs and was usually found in and around kitchens, stables or out on the streets as a basket-carrier. This original meaning still existed much later when Rinconete and Cortadillo, self-defined *pícaros* in Cervantes' tale of the same name, became 'esportilleros' ('basket-carriers') upon their arrival in Seville. It was only *c.* 1545 that *pícaro* began to take on explicitly pejorative connotations. Eugenio de Salazar's *Carta del Bachiller de Arcadia* (1548), the first reliably dated text to include the word in this sense, contrasts the 'pícaros de corte' with the 'cortesanos' ('courtiers'), referring to the former as 'ruines' ('wicked, low, vile') and to the latter as 'buenos' ('good, worthy'). Corominas correctly reminds us that implicit within this semantic shift is a change in emphasis from the *pícaro*'s social situation to his immoral and delinquent behaviour. It is interesting to note in passing that even at this early stage, the 'heroic' courtier was being confronted by the 'anti-heroic' *pícaro*, a point we will take up later.

The term *pícaro* should also be considered within the wider social and historical contexts of the sixteenth century, a period of profound social change. The Habsburg kings were committed to empire-building and waged war on a scale that the world had never seen before. Vast armies of Spanish pike-men (*picas secas* and/or *piqueros secos*, from the verb *picar*) had to be provisioned, garrisoned, transported and occasionally paid to defend Spain's far-flung territories. Geoffrey Parker has recently assessed the difficulties the Spanish military faced in the late sixteenth century:

> The increasing resort to criminals as a source of recruits can only have accentuated the innate unruliness of the troops, especially when the men were lodged in overcrowded private houses away from the supervision of their officers. The soldiers soon came to exhibit the same picaresque values which invaded Spanish society in the late sixteenth century: idleness, brutality, and bravado, the thirst for gambling, the urge for falsification. (p. 180)

The efficiency of the Spanish military decreased in the second half of the century. The change is perhaps best illustrated by the history of the wars in Flanders where Spanish troops were engaged off and on for eighty years (1587–1659). Parker states that when Don John of Austria took command of the Spanish armies in Flanders (1576), the troops had diminished in numbers from 60,000 to 11,000 men through death, disease and desertion: 'The Army had lost 80 per cent of its men in eight months' (p. 207). Deserting soldiers joined the ranks of other countries, but many attempted to return home, begging and stealing on the way. It is possible that some of the deserters carried their previous military title of *piquero* with them into 'civilian' life.

Alfonso de Pimentel, a young lieutenant who accompanied the Duke of Alba's military expedition to Flanders in 1567, wrote about his experiences in an epic poem, *Guerras civiles de Flandes* (*The Civil*

Wars of Flanders). He composed this work over twenty years later; as a result, his use of the word *pícaro* may reflect its late sixteenth-century usage. None the less, he explicitly identifies *pícaros* with the beggars he encountered during his previous military service, comparing them to the French 'gueuz' or 'guses' as he spelled the older form of *gueux*. In the context of his poem *pícaros* are real as well as false beggars. They also are viewed as evil-doers, mischief-makers and robbers. What is important about de Pimentel's remarks is not so much their connection with Flanders as the fact that most 'literary' *pícaros* become at one time or another beggars and vagrants during their careers.

In the same general region of Flanders was Picardy, a name whose Spanish form 'Picardía' was synonymous with roguery. Spanish *pícaro*, Corominas informs us, could have developed at least phonetically from French *picard* (a native of Picardy), thus possibly echoing the pattern of the Spanish word for Hungary: *Hungría/húngaro*; *Picardía/pícaro*. There is no concrete evidence that such a development took place, but the fact that both Picardy and Piedmont were traditionally the areas of Franco–Spanish conflict over many years lends some support to such an explanation. Sebastián de Covarrubias, a Spanish lexicographer of the early seventeenth century, under the heading 'Picardia' states that 'at some point a few poor people might have come from there to Spain because of their poverty, bringing us the name.'

Organized guilds of beggars were a European phenomenon, and one etymological theory of the word *pícaro* attempts to link it to the word *bigardo*, a later development of the name of a religious sect, *Pyghard*, some of whose members seemed to form a mendicant order. Such a development is especially weak – at least etymologically – when compared to the *Picardía/pícaro* explanation. There was, as we have seen, a strong and persistent semantic connection between beggars and *pícaros*. Vagrancy was not limited to northern Europe alone. Fernand Braudel eloquently describes the Spanish scene:

> In Spain, vagrants cluttered the roads, stopping at every town: students breaking bounds and forsaking their tutors to join the swelling ranks of *picardía*, adventurers of every hue, beggars

and cutpurses. They had their favourite towns and within them their headquarters: San Lucar de Barrameda, near Seville; the Slaughterhouse in Seville itself; the Puerta del Sol in Madrid. The *mendigos* formed a brotherhood, a state with its own *ferias* and sometimes met together in huge gatherings. Along the roads to Madrid moved a steady procession of poor travellers, civil servants without posts, captains without companies, humble folk in search of work, trudging behind a donkey with empty saddle bags, all faint with hunger and hoping that someone, in the capital, would settle their fate. (II, 740)

The investigations of some 'legal' historians suggest that as European society changed in the sixteenth century, attitudes toward vagrancy and criminality also changed. Even a cursory glance at the growing number and frequency of promulgated laws against criminals indicates a hardening attitude which seems to peak toward the end of the century. Joel Samaha, although dealing exclusively with Elizabethan England, points out that

> as early as the sixteenth century, contemporaries claimed that the roots of crime lay in the soil of an unstable society. Vagabonds and criminals they believed, were stamped from the same mold. Idleness bred poverty, and poverty spawned crime according to contemporary commentators – English and continental alike. Criminals, they claimed, stemmed from the poverty-stricken ranks of decayed gentlemen, uprooted peasants, ruined craftsmen, unpaid soldiers, and unemployed or underpaid laborers. (p. 112)

It is difficult, of course, to determine if reporting techniques or actual rising crime resulted in a growing awareness – and fear – of lawbreakers. Samaha suggests that both were important factors:

> Hardening community attitudes toward lawlessness, swelling ranks of law-enforcement personnel, and revamped machinery of justice have at least two meanings. They not only mean more and better records of crime, but they also represent a change in society's response to a real increase in deviance. (p. 112)

The emphasis of the picaresque on poverty, delinquency, 'upward mobility' (self-improvement of the *pícaro*), travel as an escape from despair, social satire of a system unresponsive to the needs and desires of a growing active community of 'have-nots,' all reflect the socio-historical contexts profiled by Parker, Braudel and Samaha. The 'literature of roguery' has always been of interest to literate society but it reached the proportion of an international obsession precisely at the end of the sixteenth century. As we will see, the *liber vagatorum* tradition, criminal biographies and cony-catching pamphlets found an enthusiastic audience, especially during the first half of the seventeenth century. Our special interest is with a particular kind of narrative which first appeared in mid-sixteenth-century Spain, whose full flowering as a literary genre, however, took place almost fifty years later.

The etymological, semantic, social and historical references mentioned above provide the contexts for an understanding and an appreciation of the picaresque novel, but tell us virtually nothing about it as a genre of narrative fiction. The uncertainty surrounding the origin of the word and the figure of the *pícaro* fortunately does not apply to the 'birth' of the genre itself. In 1599 Luis Sánchez, an enterprising Madrid book publisher, brought out editions of *Lazarillo de Tormes, Castigado. Agora nueuamente impresso y emendado* and of the *Primera parte de la vida de Guzmán de Alfarache, atalaya de la vida humana* (*Lazarillo de Tormes, Corrected. Now newly printed and emended*; *The First Part of the Life of Guzman de Alfarache, Watch-Tower of Man's Life*). The first book had already been published anonymously in 1554; Mateo Alemán (1547–1616?) was the author of the second.

That these narratives were seen as constituting one 'type' of fiction is established in the first part of *El ingenioso hidalgo don Quijote de la Mancha* (Madrid, 1605), chapter 22, where Cervantes has his knight-errant encounter a group of 'unfortunate ones who, much against their will, were being taken where they did not wish to go'. Sancho Panza identifies them as 'galley slaves'. Among them was one Ginés de Pasamonte, a convicted criminal who had written his autobiography during a previous sentence in the galleys. Don Quixote's interview with Ginés contains one of the earliest reactions to the then 'new' narrative genre. Don Quixote wants to

know about Ginés' life, and the rogue responds by saying
'... "If you want to know anything about my life, know that I am
Ginés de Pasamonte whose life story ['vida'] has been written down
by these fingers that you see here".' The commissary who is
guarding the prisoners intrudes to tell Don Quixote that Ginés has
'pawned' his book for 'two hundred reales', only to have Ginés
respond by placing a value on it of 'two hundred ducats'. Don
Quixote asks if the book is that valuable:

> 'It is so good,' replied Ginés, 'that it will cast into the shade
> *Lazarillo de Tormes* and all others of that sort ["género"] that
> have been or will be written. . . .'
>   'And what is the title of the book?' asked Don Quixote.
>   '*The Life of Ginés de Pasamonte*.'
>   'Is it finished?'
>   'How could it be finished,' said Ginés 'when my life is not
> finished as yet? What I have written thus far is an account of
> what happened to me from the time I was born up to the last time
> that they sent me to the galleys.' (trans. Samuel Putnam,
> Modern Library, pp. 172–3)

Within this exchange between Don Quixote and Ginés de
Pasamonte, Cervantes focuses on three fundamental elements of
Ginés' *Vida*: (1) he defines it as the autobiography of a convicted
criminal, (2) written in the pattern of *Lazarillo de Tormes* and 'all
others of that sort', and (3) he refers to its open-ended 'unfinished'
nature. A fourth element, although not specifically connected with
the autobiography itself, is the language used by criminals. In the
course of his interviews with the other prisoners, Don Quixote is
required to have translations of the thieves' cant used to describe
their misdeeds. Clearly, however, the most important words in the
encounter are contained in Ginés' statement that the written form
of his life is similar in nature to those of *Lazarillo* and others.
Ginés' status as a criminal who has given literary form to his life
while in the galleys is a thinly veiled reference to the *Guzmán de
Alfarache*, whose narrator likewise composed his autobiography
after becoming a galley slave.
  Even though the *Lazarillo* seems to have been read frequently

during the second half of the sixteenth century, it was reprinted only once, and this time in the 'chastized' or corrected version of Juan López de Velasco in 1573. As a result of this inquisitorial purification, chapters 4 and 5 were deleted along with other paragraphs and sentences containing anticlerical satire. Between 1573 and 1599 no reprints even of the corrected version were made available in Spain, an absence reflected perhaps in the remarks of the editor of the Milan 1587 edition who referred to it as 'forgotten and worm-eaten with age'. It soon found a new lease of literary life, as it were, with the publication of Alemán's *Guzmán de Alfarache*, which, in the words of Claudio Guillén, 'was one of the first authentic best sellers in the history of printing' (p. 143). Before 1605, at least twenty-five editions of the first part of Alemán's book were printed in Spain and abroad. As impressive as the public's response was to the *Guzmán*, a more important, and until recently little recognized fact, lay hidden by its popularity. The *Lazarillo* began to be reprinted, not in its original 1554 version, but in Juan de Velasco's corrected text. *Guzmán*, then, resurrected the *Lazarillo*. Luis Sánchez's 1599 edition appeared nine weeks after the first part of Alemán's novel was released for sale. Moreover, Alemán's publishers in Barcelona and Zaragoza also were selling editions of the *Lazarillo* by the end of the same year, obviously exploiting the *Guzmán*'s phenomenal success. Nine separate editions of the *Lazarillo* were in circulation by 1603. These printers and publishers were instrumental in establishing the picaresque novel as a distinct literary form in the minds of readers and authors alike at the beginning of the seventeenth century.

The picaresque novel as a genre emerges, as Cervantes clearly perceived, out of the confluence of the *Lazarillo* and of the auto-biography of a criminal. It is only through the association with the *Guzmán*, then, that the *Lazarillo* can be called a picaresque novel. But it must also be remembered that the *Lazarillo* which was 'rediscovered' in late sixteenth-century Spain is not the novel we read today. Viewing it as a 'precursor', 'prototype', or as the first picaresque novel is a reading demanded by literary history, which seeks to link it through a cluster of 'picaresque conventions' to a larger tradition. Our purpose is to review the 1554 text from the standpoint of its picaresque nature, reminding ourselves frequently that such an approach limits a full understanding and appreciation of the *Lazarillo* as a book *sui generis*.

It is only through the association with the *Guzmán* that the *Lazarillo* can be picaresque. Lazarillo, who narrates his story as the adult Lázaro, never refers to himself as a *pícaro*. How can he when he is attempting to pass himself off as a 'respectable' person, as a man of worth? There are, however, several elements which are shared by Alemán's much longer narrative and which have tended to make the *Lazarillo* a paradigm of the tradition: the first-person narration, the seemingly unstructured, episodic plot, Lazarillo's role as a 'servant of many masters', his dishonourable birth and poverty, his concern with honour and his desire for respectability, to become an 'hombre de bien'. Lázaro as narrator is a satirist, pointing out the hypocrisy of 'society' by which he is victimized. But, more importantly, he is an ironist. By overstating and emphasizing the 'sins' of others, he attempts to portray himself as a blameless man, no better, but certainly no worse than his neighbours.

Lazarillo de Tormes: epistolary beginnings of the picaresque

Lázaro's *Vida* is written in the form of an epistle. He has been asked by an unknown person, simply referred to as 'vuestra merced' ('your grace', 'your honour'), to respond to rumours that are circulating in the city of Toledo concerning his unseemly behaviour. It has come to 'your grace's' attention that Lázaro is a willing participant in a *ménage-à-trois*: his wife is the local arch-priest's concubine. Lázaro's response is his autobiography. He insists that in order to show 'your grace' how he managed to find himself in such a situation, which he calls a 'caso' ('case', 'matter'), he must begin at the beginning, that is, he must narrate his experiences from birth to his final 'present' position in life. In essence, the oral language of gossip threatens his comfortable life, and in order to protect himself he resorts to a written response as his ultimate defence. He becomes an author.

Lázaro is the son of a thief and a woman of questionable morals. He was born in a mill on the river Tormes which flows beside the university city of Salamanca. Forced to leave home when his father dies and his mother is no longer able to support him, he is turned over to a blind beggar who treats him cruelly. It is through the beggar's cruelty that young Lazarillo learns to fend for himself. He begins as a simpleton, naïve in the ways of the world, and is violently and abruptly brought out of his simplicity by letting the blind beggar smash his head against a stone bull. At the end of the chapter he pays in kind by tricking the beggar into jumping into a stone pillar, a feat he accomplishes by becoming a clever liar. Thereafter he immediately takes up with a miserly priest who nearly starves him to death. Lazarillo attempts to use his recently developed art as a liar against the priest. Hunger has driven him to steal from the priest's chest of 'holy' bread, and after inventing a story which blames the steadily increasing thefts on rats, he is able to satisfy his appetite at will. His success is his undoing. After obtaining a key to the chest from a travelling tinker, he hides it in his mouth at night for safe-keeping. While he is sleeping one night, his breath passes through its opening, awakening the priest. Lazarillo pays for his unwitting mistake as his master pummels him half to death. His third master, a squire, values honour above all things. Lazarillo believes at first that he has found a good master who will provide him with food and shelter. He discovers, however, that the squire's honour consists only in his honourable appearance. And now that his hunger is more intense than before, he is reduced to begging for both his master and himself. He learns that honour exists in the eyes of the beholder only and that an illusion of respectability and worth functions well as long as the fiction can be sustained. For the first time in his life, Lazarillo is abandoned by his master as the squire skips town when his true worth is learned.

Lazarillo's other masters are a Mercedarian friar, a fraudulent pardoner, a tambourine painter, a cathedral chaplain in Toledo and a constable. Gradually he becomes his own man by working for himself rather than for others. First he enters into a contract with the chaplain who puts him in charge of a donkey, four jugs and a whip, and Lazarillo earns enough money after four years – and after paying his expenses – to buy a 'good secondhand suit of clothes' (p. 93). Later he becomes the constable's assistant but finds the work too dangerous when he is chased by some escaped criminals. Finally he attains the position of town crier in Toledo 'with the help of some friends and other people' (p. 95), thus reaching the 'height' of his good fortune. Still not satisfied, he agrees to marry the archpriest's 'maid' because he has realized that 'good and profitable things could come from a man like him' (p. 98). But almost immediately Lazarillo becomes the object of gossip and scorn. The novel ends at this point, coming full circle in the sense that he has married a woman like his mother and is still at the mercy of another, the archpriest, and above him, 'your grace'.

Lázaro's life has been described as the story of a young boy growing into manhood. His struggles reveal the hypocrisy of a certain sector of society from the 'outside'. It is told in a humorous, sometimes bitter tone, but in the end, as paradoxical as it may seem, Lázaro emerges as the master and society as the slave because he is the one who manipulates the language and selects the episodes with which to narrate his life. While the novel may be partly drawn from folk literature (the blind beggar and his servant) or from Italian fiction (the fifth chapter is said to be taken from Masuccio Salernitano's *Il Novellino*), it is in its totality a 'new' kind of fiction both in execution and meaning. In R. O. Jones' words:

> No previous narrative offers what this one does: a portrait of a child in the process of becoming a man, an account of how he is moulded imperceptibly by the example of others, so that when we realise with a shock that his childish innocence has gone for good we cannot decide when and where the change took place. (p. 71)

The process of Lazarillo's growth to manhood is indeed a 'new' subject for fiction, but as previously mentioned, his autobiography is also 'new' in the sense that it simultaneously tells the story of how he becomes an author. In the Prologue to his report to 'your grace', Lázaro contrasts two kinds of honour. The first is that which comes with noble birth and lineage and belongs to those who are favoured by fortune. The other is that which can be earned through hard work and merit. Lázaro's questionable ancestry denies him inherited honour, and so through misfortune he falls into the second category. But is there honour in this other direction? The author of the *Lazarillo* is reformulating a Spanish Renaissance debate about honour which was most clearly outlined by Antonio de Torquemada in his *Colloquios satíricos* (Mondoñedo, 1553), a very influential work of the time. Torquemada asks which is the 'truest honour, that which is gained through valour and merit or that which proceeds from one's ancestors?' His answer is that honour comes from virtue and not from appearances or self-esteem. 'Bad' honour is the opposite of Christian humility and should be avoided at all costs. Lázaro, in his own perverse way, thinks likewise except for the important fact that 'virtue' for him is defined as that which profits him most. 'Honra y provecho' ('honour and profit') go hand in hand in Lázaro's world. The orthodox concepts of good and evil are turned inside out.

Lázaro invokes the name of Cicero to support his view that honour can be earned. He will in effect become another Cicero in attempting to gain praise and fame by writing his book. With tongue in cheek he seeks the 'good' honour of Torquemada because writing is after all hard work, as he explicitly states in the Prologue:

... writing is hardly a simple thing to do. But since writers go ahead with it, they want to be rewarded, not with money but with people seeing and reading their works, and if there is something worthwhile in them, they would like some praise. (p. 3)

It is not a coincidence that Cicero's name is mentioned in this context. In Torquemada's *Colloquios*, as Fernando Lázaro Carreter recently reminded us, one of the interlocutors brings up Sallust's accusation that Cicero came from 'low and obscure ancestors and from modest and unworthy parents'. Cicero's alleged response, according to Torquemada, was that the 'virtue' of his works had produced his famous reputation and because of this he was worthy of more honour than those who had inherited it. This is precisely Lázaro's situation, for not only will he save himself from the rumours, but simultaneously he will gain an even 'higher' Ciceronian honour by writing his book. The phrase quoted by Lázaro in the Prologue, 'honour promotes the arts', is reversed to mean that Lázaro's artistry will create his honour.

In order to become like Cicero, Lázaro must acquire the art of the orator, of the manipulator of language. If we look beneath the surface of his 'picaresque' adventures, we find that each of them teaches him something different about the nature of language, especially oral language. From the blind beggar he learns the magic quality of words: they produce money from unsuspecting alms-givers. From the priest who says mass everyday, Lazarillo perceives that his 'sacred' words bring forth money as well as food. From the squire he learns that honour is as 'real' as the language used to create it. But the most important lesson he learns is from the pardoner, whose salesmanship involves 'all sorts of ruses and under-handed tricks' (p. 81). In essence, the pardoner is a salesman who has mastered completely the art of speaking and persuasion. His ecclesiastical rhetoric is so polished that through a series of care-fully staged tricks and a masterfully delivered sermon, his congrega-tion is totally deceived into buying his pardons. The fame of one of his false miracles spreads to neighbouring villages where the local 'naïve' populace is waiting to be deceived into massive purchases.

This episode has been called superfluous to the novel. It is, on the contrary, central to Lázaro's intention to 'sell' his book to 'your grace'. Lázaro, like the pardoner, faces a sceptical audience. If he is unsuccessful in obtaining the sympathy and support of 'your grace', he will have no defence against the ugly but true rumours of his neighbours in Toledo. His problem is how to acknowledge the truth of these rumours yet escape their con-sequences by portraying himself as the innocent victim of his past experiences. His understanding of the power of language is put to its ultimate test. While disclosing but simultaneously 'blinding' the reader into accepting his dishonourable situation, he is able to sell himself and thus to survive. His own written text is analogous to the papal indulgence in that it too produces blindness while communicating the truth of its fiction.

The real purpose of Lázaro's autobiography is clear. 'Your grace' is not interested in the lowly town crier out of mere curiosity. He is concerned with his own honour. The archpriest of San Salvador is his 'friend and servant' (p. 98), Lázaro notes; he is also Lázaro's friend and business partner. Lázaro implies – and not very subtly – that 'your grace' is involved in the scandal by association, and if he cares for his reputation, he will put an end to the gossip. The complicity woven by Lázaro's linguistic artistry points to the 'reality' of a social order which exists only on a foundation of deceit and fraud. If 'truth' were allowed to survive, the social structure would collapse under its weight. Lázaro's discovery of language as the basis of social reality is also his discovery of the full implication of himself as the 'voice' of Toledo. We are no more, no less, than the language we speak and write.

Lázaro's attempt to remake society in his own image is a logical but perverse development of the Renaissance idea of the 'dignity of man'. His gift of speech, while indeed defining him as a man, is manipulated to insert him in a community so obsessed with honour and appearance that it is unable to see the illusory nature of its value system. Lázaro's self-willed deception at the end of the novel places him firmly in such a society, but his irony and cynicism communicated through his language guarantee his ability to manipulate those around him as he has manipulated his *Vida*. Such a cynical view of life will become one of the fundamental hallmarks of later *pícaro*-authors.

Literary historians continue to debate whether or not the sudden appearance of a book like the *Lazarillo* was a reaction to the Greek, chivalric and pastoral romances which flourished at about the same time, that is, whether the *Lazarillo* constitutes a 'counter genre' within the framework of sixteenth-century Spanish fiction. Historians especially persist in evaluating it as a social document which allegedly reproduces to one degree or another the 'reality' of the age preceding Spain's political and economic decline. As we have seen, however, it was Cervantes who first placed the *Lazarillo* in its proper *literary*-historical perspective at the turn of the seventeenth century. And it was the *Guzmán de Alfarache* which provided Cervantes with the context to enable him to see the *Lazarillo* as part of a larger tradition.

Mateo Alemán: the picaresque as genre

In 1593 Mateo Alemán was appointed by the Crown to investigate reports that galley slaves were being mistreated in the quicksilver mines of Almadén. Part of his final report to the government was probably based on face-to-face interviews with the prisoners. This experience must have left a lasting impression, for in 1598 we find him corresponding with Cristóbal Pérez de Herrera, one of the most important social reformers of the time. Pérez de Herrera was concerned with the widespread poverty and vagrancy in Spain, a problem he had attempted to alleviate for several years. Out of his work came the famous *Discurso del amparo de los legítimos pobres* (*Dissertation on the Protection of Genuine Paupers*), Madrid, 1598. Alemán's letter included references to what had already been done to help the poor, but more relevant for our purpose, he mentioned that when he revealed the tricks of false beggars in the *Guzmán*, his primary interest was to call the public's attention to the plight of real paupers who were in desperate need of help. Alemán's first-hand knowledge of prison life, his interviews with the Almadén galley slaves and his close association with serious efforts to deal with poverty supplied him with ample 'raw' data for his narrative. That he used any of this material is a disputed point. In any case his major problem was to structure it into a literary work, to give it 'form'. His recourse to the *Lazarillo* as a model is often accepted as fact, although there is no hard evidence that he had it in mind when he began the composition of the *Guzmán*.

Alemán divided and published his novel in two parts (1599, 1604), each consisting of three books. The symmetry reflected in the arrangement of chapters, books and parts extends to the 'content' of the narrative as well. The first part traces Guzmán's progress from birth to his chosen career as a *pícaro*. The second takes up where he refuses to mend his ways, includes his steadily worsening situation – the high point of his life as a delinquent – and ends with his arrest, punishment and 'repentance' of past crimes. Another structuring element of the novel is its narrative viewpoint. Because the *Guzmán* is an autobiography like the *Lazarillo*, there are two temporal perspectives, one serving as a framework for the other. Guzmán, the much older narrator, recounts his past life as a character. The entire book consists of 'picaresque' episodes, but they are punctuated with the narrator's digressions and commentaries. According to another viewpoint, however, these 'interruptions' exist first and are illustrated by examples, that is, by the picaresque adventures. These viewpoints have generated two interpretations of the reading of the novel. On the one hand, the *Guzmán* has been considered as principally an 'immoral' work whose adventures revel in the humour and the 'low' life of the *pícaro*. On the other hand, the work has been described as moralistic, praising the 'good' life by condemning Guzmán's delinquent behaviour as a character. If we are what Alemán calls the 'discreto lector' ('enlightened reader'), we should penetrate the humour and entertainment of the picaresque episodes to profit from the serious didactic intention of the book. If, on the other hand, we are, or choose to be, the 'vulgo lector' ('unenlightened reader', overly critical), we concentrate on Guzmán's roguish life without extracting more than vicarious pleasure.

Despite several efforts to establish one reading over the other, the 'correct' interpretation remains ambiguous. Some readers insist on seeing Guzmán's final penitence in an ironic light, claiming that his stated intention to change his life is simply another picaresque lie. His decision to be a virtuous person in the last chapter is a trick to escape from the galleys and not self-reform. However, it is most likely, based on what we know about Alemán's life, his concern for social reform and his Counter-Reformation attitudes, that Guzmán's repentance is to be taken seriously. Whatever the genuine interpretation may be, the book was and is still read in both ways. Soon after its publication, readers referred to it as the *Libro del pícaro*, indicating that a considerable seventeenth-century audience was not as concerned with its moral values and doctrinal teachings as with its implied invitation to live vicariously the life of a rogue. Alemán, in the introduction to the second part, admitted that his book had been so 'misread', and possibly as a consequence, the second part contains many more 'moral' digressions than the first.

The *Guzmán*, like the *Lazarillo*, is on the surface the story of a lad born in dishonourable circumstances who attempts to better his position in life. He was born in San Juan de Alfarache near Seville, the illegitimate son of a renegade Christian and a woman of easy virtue. After his father's death, poverty forces Guzmán to make his way to Madrid. He takes part in several 'picaresque' exploits during the journey and arrives 'hecho pícaro', already a rogue.

Guzmán's role as a *pícaro* in Madrid is of special significance. This is the first time in any literary text that the figure of the *pícaro* as such is given a full description and definition. Chapter 2 of Book II begins with the following summary, as translated by James Mabbe: 'How Guzman de Alfarache leaving his Host, went begging to Madrid; and comming thither, how he set himselfe to learne to play the Rogue, and to beare a Basket; where by the way he discourseth of Hunger, of Beggerie; and of Honour which hurteth the soule' (I, 249). The 'Host' to whom Guzmán refers is his master until he decides to leave him because he 'was no better (to speake the best of it) than an Inne-keepers Boy, which is some-what worse than a blind-man' (*ibid.*). Mabbe's translation of the final part of Guzmán's remark unfortunately is incorrect. The Spanish text reads: 'era mozo de ventero, que es peor que de ciego' (ed. F. Rico, p. 257). Guzmán says in reality that he was an innkeeper's boy which is worse than being a blindman's servant, thus seeming to echo Lazarillo's initial adventure. Whether or not Alemán consciously alludes to the *Lazarillo* is impossible to say, but it is remarkable that Lazarillo's life as a beggar's assistant is the starting point of Guzmán's career as a *pícaro*.

Guzmán quickly spends the money he has 'gotten in a good warre', is forced to beg, and is ultimately required to sell the clothes off his back. His clothing is especially important to him because it identifies him in the eyes of others: '. . . when I came to Madrid, I look't like one that had come from the Oare, or some gentile Rower returned lately from the Gallies, I was so lightly clad . . .' (I, 250). Guzmán, as the 'petitent' thief and galley slave writing his own life, compares himself to what he will eventually become. He can find no employment because he looks like a criminal: 'They did thinke, that I was some roguish little Thiefe, and that if they should take me in, I would filch some thing from them, and betake mee to my heeles when I had done' (I, 251). But Guzmán is not officially a *pícaro* yet. Only after seeing his desperate state does he begin to 'follow the Trade *de la Florida Picardía*' (*ibid.*), which consists in 'exercising all your Cony-catching trickes, knavish prankes, fine feates, with slight of hand, and whatsoever Rogueries come within the compasse of that prowling office' (*ibid.*). Some of these 'feates' include standing in soup lines for free meals, learning to be a card-sharper, stealing, and carrying baskets. He exults in his freedom, serving only himself for the most part without having to engage in hard physical labour:

> What a fine kind of life was it, what a dainty and delicate thing, without Thimble, Thred, or Needle; without Pinsers, Hammer, or Wimble, or any other Mechanicall Instrument whatsoever, more than one onely bare Basket; like unto those of your Brethren of the Order de Anton Martin, (though unlike to them in their goodnesse of life, and solitary retiredness) I had gotten me an Office whereby to live: and such a kind of Office, as seemed to be a bit without a bone; a backe, without a burthen; a merry kind of Occupation, and free from all manner of trouble and vexation. (I, 254)

Guzmán survives at the expense of society. He is a parasite, complaining of the great burden of honour, 'vaine' honour, in whose name men sacrifice their lives. It is the older Guzmán, however, whose voice both criticizes the honour-monger and praises the man 'that neither knowes what Honour meanes, nor seekes after it, nor hath any thing to do with this Titulary toy' (I, 255).

The young Guzmán soon leaves for Toledo where he buys elegant clothing and attempts to pass himself off as a gentleman of means. But he is quickly found out and is forced to leave. Later he joins a group of soldiers and decides to accompany them to Italy where he intends to make the acquaintance of his father's 'noble' and wealthy relatives in Genoa. They see through his schemes and cast him out. Afterwards, Guzmán is worse off than ever and takes up his earlier profession as a beggar on his way to Rome. He learns all kinds of tricks to extract money from unsuspecting victims, one of whom, a cardinal, takes pity on his false wounds and invites him to be his servant. Guzmán steals from the cardinal, promptly losing his money by gambling it away. The cardinal is the only good master he has had and he rejects him in favour of working for the French ambassador, whose immoral life is more to Guzmán's liking. At this point Alemán inserts an Italianate tale into the narrative, bringing the 1599 first part to a close.

In the second part, Guzmán serves the ambassador well but fails when he attempts to emulate his master's success with women.

Leaving Rome, he passes through Florence, Siena, Bologna and Milan on his return to Genoa. Along the way he amasses a good fortune through theft and trickery and returns to Genoa where he takes vengeance on his relatives and departs for Spain. In Madrid he becomes a merchant and marries but loses both his wife and his fortune. Guzmán travels to Alcalá de Henares to study for the priesthood at the university. His intention is far from religious; he chooses the priestly life to find material security. This career also fails. After marrying a prostitute who subsequently abandons him, he returns to Seville where he is caught stealing from his final employer, a wealthy woman. Guzmán is arrested, convicted and sentenced to the galleys. While serving his time, he 'repents' and determines to live a virtuous life from that point onward. He now writes the memoirs of his finished criminal life.

Alemán's *pícaro* differs radically from Lazarillo de Tormes. Lazarillo is never a hardened criminal. The only time he breaks the law is when he is forced to beg to feed himself and the squire. This criminal activity is minimal compared to the countless thefts and frauds perpetrated by Guzmán. Guzmán serves many more masters than does Lazarillo. Both characters attend the 'school of hard knocks,' but Guzmán receives a formal university education, 'having (by his study) come to be a good Latinist, Rhetorician, and Grecian ... [going] ... forward in his Studies, with purpose to professe the state of Religion' (Alemán in 'A Declaration for the Better Understanding of this Booke,' I, 19). Alemán educates Guzmán to justify the 'Tracts of Doctrine' he puts in his mouth. Alemán also enlarges the world of his rogue. Lazarillo travels from Salamanca to Toledo; Guzmán's itinerary takes him from Seville, across Spain, through Italy to Rome. Not only are some of the major themes of the *Lazarillo* modified and expanded, but its size and scope under Alemán's pen grow to mammoth proportions. In Francisco Rico's recent edition of both works, the *Lazarillo* fills seventy-five pages whereas the *Guzmán* extends to eight hundred and twenty. The *Guzmán* is encyclopedic in a Renaissance sense too. Its narrative is inflated with learned discourses, esoteric knowledge (a discussion of the Pythagorean 'Y', for instance), interpolated Italianate novels and an extensive series of satires against money, honour, justice and a multitude of social types: women, judges, notaries, lawyers, doctors, bankers, innkeepers, false beggars, to name only a few. Nearly all this material, as well as the 'Tracts of Doctrine', is contained in Guzmán's digressions.

Alemán, unlike the author of the *Lazarillo*, does not consistently feature the shortcomings of the Roman Catholic Church. Some readers have suggested that since Guzmán's 'conversion' is a religious one, and that since the cardinal is virtually the only 'good' character in the novel, Alemán eschews critical commentary on those abuses described in the *Lazarillo*. With its heavy emphasis on the doctrines of original sin, the saving power of grace and the concept of free will, Maurice Molho has described the novel not as the 'life' of a criminal, but as the 'life' of a criminal's soul. In this interpretation the Guzmán can indeed be called a 'confession' structured around a worldly 'pilgrimage' with Rome as the spiritual destination. However, this religious and moral framework of the *Guzmán* should not be over-stressed. It may be a moral work without being doctrinally dogmatic because, as J. A. Jones has recently argued, 'it attempts to draw attention to basic conflicts and tensions of human life, and tries to establish the need for individuals and for society in general to confront these problems by constant adherence to truthful and responsible behaviour' (*Knaves and Swindlers*, p. 46). In a 'secular' vein, Alemán's obsessive attack on what could be called loosely a budding 'bourgeois' society concentrates on the corrupting power of money on all those persons associated with it: merchants, bankers, lawyers and the 'nobility'. From this perspective, Molho has called the book a 'violent anti-capitalist indictment, without doubt the most violent that sixteenth- and seventeenth-century aristocratic Europe produced against money, banking and commerce . . .' (p. xiv). The *pícaro*, as Alemán defines him, is the product of poverty and of a social value system which prohibits him from being anything else. Both Lazarillo's and Guzmán's real crimes were having been born into the world as 'losers', doomed to failure from the beginning in their attempts to create and to sustain that myth of 'honour' for which they sacrificed their spiritual lives.

Spanish descendants of the 'Lazarillo' and the 'Guzmán'

It was the combined popularity and publication of the *Lazarillo* and the *Guzmán* which generated imitations, emulations and parodies of the new genre. The first part of the *Guzmán* was followed by a 'false' second part, written by 'Mateo Luján de Sayavedra, native of Seville'. In reality Luján was the Valencian lawyer, Juan Martí. Martí published his sequel in Valencia in 1602, immediately capturing the audience created by Alemán. Between 1602 and 1603 fourteen editions were printed, only one appearing in 1604, the year Alemán's second part was published in Lisbon. In short, Martí exploited the *Guzmán*'s instant success, apparently to make a quick profit from the explosive rise of the picaresque. He clearly intended his work to be read as the continuation promised by Alemán's first part. For instance, in order to identify and to confuse his novel with Alemán's, he called it *Segunda parte del Guzmán de Alfarache*. The name he created for his narrator ('Mateo') was an obvious attempt to connect the sequel to Alemán himself. Martí also reproduced the formal structure of the original by dividing his continuation into three books. Moreover, he began Guzmán's adventures at the point where Alemán had left his rogue 'suspended' in Rome. Mateo Luján refers to this 'continuing' adventure with the French ambassador: 'my life with the French ambassador was not satisfactory because, as I said, he only cared for his own pleasure, not my profit'. The insertion 'as I said' refers to a previous remark made by the 'real' Guzmán towards the end of the first part. Martí's intention, with one or two exceptions, was to continue the novel so that his audience would detect few if any differences in theme or structure.

In Martí's version the narrative perspective of a 'penitent' criminal who judges his past life is absent. An escaped convict, his picaresque activities simply reflect the episodic structure of his life and lead to no conclusion. Martí preserves the right of his narrator to digress, indeed, as the novel unfolds, the narration of the picaresque episodes diminishes as the digressions expand. Martí was not as interested in the complex relationships between his rogue's picaresque adventures and digressions as he was in using this structure to lard his narrative with plagiarized episodes and sermons and 'touristic' descriptions of famous places and people. Alemán's reaction to what he considered to be Martí's distortion of his own work was predictable. Much of the authentic part of the *Guzmán* is taken up with references to Martí as a 'thief', worse than his own rogue. Alemán takes vengeance by having Guzmán meet Mateo Lugán's brother and witness his drowning. Finally, Martí's pointless repetition of Guzmán's adventures establishes an open-ended and frameless imitation of experience without the structuring control of art. It is this quality that Cervantes criticizes in the Ginés de Pasamonte episode of *Don Quixote* and to which he returns in three of his 'exemplary' tales: *Rinconete y Cortadillo*, *La ilustre fregona* (*The Illustrious Kitchen-Maid*) and the *Coloquio de los perros* (*The Dogs' Colloquy*).

The picaresque novel was firmly established as a literary genre with Martí's imitation. This period also ends the first phase of the history of the genre in Spain. Cervantes' reaction to a fictional autobiography which pretended to be true was one of the first negative criticisms. His concern with the interaction between fiction and reality is well known. And his obsession with both the influence fiction had on life and vice-versa is a commonplace of literary history. *Don Quixote* is certainly his longest, most ironic, and yet in some ways, his most serious statement on the subject. He was convinced that reading 'good' fiction was a valid way of spending leisure time. Hence the author of fictions had a serious responsibility in dealing with his readers' responses to the powerful illusory nature of literature. From the viewpoint of Cervantes' literary aesthetic, the subject of the picaresque novel – a criminal, hypocritical life told by the *pícaro* himself – was never allowed to exist by itself without a larger context. It had to be contained within a fictional framework and its fictional nature had to be constantly pointed out to his readers. For Cervantes there were 'born' *pícaros* as well as picaresque masks that could be put on by anyone at will. Rinconete and Cortadillo, for example, are born rogues who tell each other their exploits and who embody the wandering nature of *pícaros* subject only to fortune and will. They end up in Seville in a society of adult thieves headed by the master-thief, Monipodio. What they and we discover is that the freedom, unstructured and uncontrolled life, for which they live is an illusion. They find that the thieves' society is based on a constraining hierarchy, kept in place at every level by their own rules and those of the 'outside' society. They leave Seville only to continue their wandering and unstable, floating existence which points to an experience ended by death rather than by art.

In *The Illustrious Kitchen-Maid*, two lads of noble blood attempt to drop their responsibilities in society to enjoy the life of picaresque freedom. After living roguish lives they return to their proper places and roles as aristocrats. Here the picaresque experience is viewed as a parenthetical moment in their lives, a space in which to 'live out' illusory desires by shedding their former identities. *The Dogs' Colloquy* is an ironic portrayal of the picaresque experience. Two dogs suddenly find that they possess the power of speech. They spend the night during which one tells the other of his picaresque life as a dog-servant of many masters. Their dialogue 'exists' in the dream or vision of a soldier (hence its doubly fictional nature) who is being treated for syphilis. Cervantes places several allusions in their conversation to contemporary picaresque narratives – primarily to the *Guzmán* – humorously undercutting the picaresque novel's claim to portray accurately the 'human' experiences of a rogue or to stand as an autonomous art-form. The autobiographical viewpoint of the genre with its narrow – sometimes 'criminal' – interpretation of experience was too dogmatic to fit into Cervantes' assessment of the serious nature and responsibility that literature should bear.

Cervantes' considerations of the serious implications of the picaresque from the standpoint of both literature and experience seem to be unique. His attitude was certainly not shared by the authors of picaresque novels which were written soon after the publication of *Guzmán de Alfarache*. In 1605 the first novel to feature a *pícara*, a female rogue, was published in Medina del Campo. It was called *Libro de entretenimiento de la pícara Justina* (*The Entertaining Life of the Rogue Justine*) and written by a physician from Toledo, Francisco López de Ubeda. There is no doubt that it was conceived in the mould of the *Guzman*. Justina, already having been married several times, is about to contract another marriage with

Guzmán himself. The first edition contains an engraving which 'visually' establishes the connection between Justina's experiences and those of Guzmán and of Lazarillo. It depicts two boats, the larger one inscribed as 'The Ship of the Picaresque Life', which bears 'Mother Celestina', 'Justina' and 'Guzman'. It is towed by another boat which is rowed by 'Lazarillo' towards the 'Port of Death' ('desengaño').

La pícara Justina is a burlesque of the recent novels of Alemán and Martí. It is also a *roman-á-clef* in that López de Ubeda uses the 'life' of a *pícara* to satirize several 'real' persons in residence at the Court. (The Spanish Court was removed to Valladolid from Madrid in 1601 where it remained until 1606.) The novel opens with Justina attempting to write down the outline of her family history when she is interrupted by a young jester ('licentiate Perlícaro') who resembles in appearance and attitude Francisco de Quevedo. He introduces a major theme of the novel when he accuses her of coming from a family of converted Jews ('conversos'). López de Ubeda includes other famous and not-so-famous persons and authors in his veiled references. He also satirizes activities of Philip III himself when turning Justina into a pilgrim and taking her to the city of León. Philip III made a pilgrimage to this city in 1602, and on the basis of López de Ubeda's references, Marcel Bataillon has been able to date the composition of this part of the novel between 1602 and 1603. Finding allusions to Alemán's second part of the *Guzmán*, Bataillon further concludes that the writing of Justina's 'life' ends sometime in 1604.

López de Ubeda divides his *pícara*'s autobiography into four books, each treating a different phase in her career. The first is called the 'pícara montañesa' ('highlander rogue'), an obvious and clever reference on the part of the author to Justina's attempt to identify herself and her ancestry with 'old Christian' stock, untainted with Jewish blood. The second book is concerned with the 'pícara romera' ('pilgrim rogue') in which Justina takes a trip to the city of León in imitation of Philip III's then recent journey. She satirizes and pokes fun at León's Gothic architecture, calling attention to its ugly and ancient churches, monuments and palaces. In the third book she becomes the 'pícara pleitista' ('pettifogger rogue') and returns to 'Ríoseco' (in reality, Madrid) to bring suit against an unscrupulous mayor and her own family for depriving her of an inheritance. They turn out to be Moriscos and Justina victimizes them by stealing their oil and wool, tricks that would have delighted an audience who applauded a few years later the expulsion of such people. In the fourth book she is the 'pícara novia' ('betrothed rogue'), describing the premarital adventures which lead to her engagement to Guzman.

While *La pícara Justina* shares many of the picaresque conventions of its predecessors such as the autobiographical viewpoint, the theme of 'honour' and a satiric view of society, it remains a private work whose full meaning is reserved for relatively few readers. López de Ubeda speaks from behind the skirts of his rogue to mock with brilliant turns of phrase, puns, allusions and blunt statements the contemporary obsession with 'purity of blood'. Justina is not a servant to any master except to her author, who takes her where he can find the most pertinent objects for his vicious satire. She is more a court buffoon than a rogue. López de Ubeda's transformation of the *pícaro* in this direction marks an important change in the figure of the rogue which is taken up by his contemporary, Quevedo, who was working on his *Buscón* at the same time, and much later by the *pícaro* Estebanillo González (1646), who became the court jester of Ottavio Piccolomini, Duke of Amalfi.

Francisco de Quevedo (1580–1645) traced his genealogy back to the 'Goths', that is, to the most ancient, noble and pure-blooded Spaniards. He was concerned with preserving the authentic nobility, with protecting its blood, status and reputation, and his conservative attitude is obvious in *La vida del Buscón, llamado don Pablos*, the autobiography of Pablos who seeks to ascend the social ladder through deceit and trickery only to be exposed publicly and cruelly punished for his 'high-minded', presumptuous thoughts. Quevedo's message is clear. Pablos is forced to wander as a hardened, obstinate criminal, accompanied only by the prostitute with whom he has chosen to live at the end of the novel. He is condemned to relive his father's life.

Pablos, like the other *pícaros* we have mentioned, is born into a family of thieves. His father is a barber who 'shaves' men's pockets; his younger brother is beaten to death in jail. Pablos' mother is a prostitute and witch who is arrested by the Inquisition and sentenced to be burned at the stake. His uncle is the town executioner of his native city, Segovia. Despite such an environment, Pablos has 'high' thoughts of improving himself and becoming a gentleman. He receives his early formal education from Cabra ('Goat'), a symbol of the devil, who almost starves Pablos and his boyhood 'friend' Don Diego to death. He later attends the University of Alcalá, where he spends half his time being spat upon and wallowing in his defecation-filled bed, the other half in joining those who persecuted him as a petty thief and general practical joker. He returns home to collect an inheritance, like all 'gentlemen', which is surely the money his father had managed to steal during his infamous career. He goes to Madrid and on the way meets 'don Toribio Rodríguez Vallejo Gómez de Ampuero y Jordán', a 'gentleman' of the Court who tells Pablos about his easy life. Already in his career Pablos has met, among others, a poet-cleric, a political schemer, a fencing master, a card-playing hermit, and a boasting soldier. He has exposed all of them through his satire. In Madrid he is inducted into a society of thieves, obtains proper clothing, associates with real gentlemen, and makes his fatal mistake in trying to marry into a respectable family. The girl he is courting is his boyhood friend Don Diego's cousin. Don Diego reveals Pablos' true identity, 'son of a whore and thief', and arranges to have his face slashed to mark him for life. But Quevedo ironically undercuts even Diego's status as a gentleman by identifying him at the beginning of the novel as a member of the notorious Coronel family, descendants of the converted Jew, Abraham Coronel of Segovia.

Pablos finds 'success' both as a false beggar and as an actor and producer of plays. He functions well in the doubly fictional world of the stage. Yet he gives up this career and goes to Seville where he joins a band of criminals, and in a state of extreme inebriation, is involved in the murder of a constable. Finding temporary refuge in the Cathedral of Seville, where he also finds Grajales, a prostitute who 'earns' her living in the same edifice, he leaves with her in search of a better life and better luck.

The relatively clear and straightforward plot of the *Buscón* is at times difficult to follow because of the 'dense' nature of Quevedo's language. The effort involved in deciphering these tricks of language is further complicated by the various types and levels of language used by Quevedo to write the book. Pablos and the other characters speak to us in thieves' cant, liturgical and medical vocabulary, pseudo-scientific jargon, the language of lyric poetry, military slang, the terminology of card-playing, gestures and songs of beggars and the language of political bureaucracy. Quevedo's linguistic virtuosity and the overall Court-centred nature of the book have led many readers to see it as nothing more than a 'libro de entretenimiento' ['joke book'] in the mould of *La pícara Justina*. As such it contains no moral concern or relevance. Seen from the viewpoint of the *Guzmán*'s explicit religious orthodoxy, this assessment is true. But within the context of Quevedo's other, Neostoic writings, the *Buscón*'s morality is satiric and social in nature. Henry Ettinghausen has convincingly shown that 'Pablos is portrayed as the antithesis of the Stoic sage, an example of and a warning to the *vulgus*' (p. 127). Pablos' background and pride threaten the values of a society based on 'noble' blood, and, ideally on Christian humility and obedience.

Another picaresque novel written at about the same time (*c*. 1604) but edited only recently is Gregorio González's *El guitón Honofre*. The word *guitón* in the title is synonomous with *pícaro*. Contemporary dictionaries define it more specifically as a false beggar of foreign origin who visits holy places, feigning poverty in order to collect alms and fóod. But Honofre explicitly rejects the life of a beggar, choosing instead to become a gentleman. His surname in Spanish, 'Caballero', means gentleman. But González, who seems to be a real gentleman, takes the attitude of Quevedo by preventing his rogue from attaining his goal. Thus *El guitón Honofre* is conceived and written more in the pattern of the *Lazarillo* and the *Buscón* than of the *Guzmán* of Alemán.

González tells us that he wrote the book to amuse himself while recovering from an unspecified illness. His stated intention, then, was to produce a work of entertainment for himself and his friends. The novel seems to bear out such a 'recreational' motivation. The primary motif repeated throughout the novel is vengeance, the vengeance that Honofre takes on his various masters. He is born into poverty and is orphaned after the death of his peasant parents ('labradores'). Taken in by a widower, Honofre is treated cruelly by the housekeeper. He responds in kind by placing sharp stones in the spot where she is accustomed to sitting. He becomes the servant of a sacristan and then serves a student at the University of Salamanca. The student becomes a priest, and Honofre is left to fend for himself. His tricks and jokes lead to more serious 'criminal' behaviour. After a successful postal fraud, he attempts to pose as a tax-collector. He is discovered and thrown into prison but manages to escape through clever exploitation of the judicial system. This leads him to say that 'sinners' go free while 'good' but poor people pay the penalty for such corruption. In the final chapter Honofre convinces a Dominican prior that he should be admitted as a sincere convert to the order. His feigned penitence is motivated by his desire to escape punishment. And in the final sentence of his 'life' he promises a second part which will feature a detailed account of his 'priestly' adventures together with a renunciation of his illicitly acquired religious habit.

González uses the conventions of the new genre to construct his narrative, excepting, of course, the final conversion of the rogue, thus leaving the *Guzmán* of Alemán as the only picaresque novel which presents a 'penitent' narrator. This early phase of the genre includes both the creation of the picaresque novel *sensu strictu* and the beginnings of its dissolution into the picaresque in a looser sense. *La pícara Justina*, *El buscón*, and *El guitón Honofre* adapt both the 'outer' formal elements such as the first-person narration, auto-biographical form, dishonourable birth of the 'hero', and the motifs of poverty, hunger, delinquency and the *pícaro* as a servant of many masters. These works also adapt a loose 'inner' form, namely, the goal of the *pícaro* to better his material and social situation. But it was precisely in the adaptation of these elements that they lost their original functions, and in so doing became 'empty' conventions. The *pícaro* in these works often becomes a satirist while simultaneously being the satiric object of the real author: 'the man who pretended, appeared, or even believed himself to be part of society, to be pious or rich, a doctor or poet [and "gentleman" we should add] while actually being an interloper from beyond the pale' (Paulson, *Satire and the Novel*, p. 5).

The picaresque novel after Cervantes

Further publications of 'new' picaresque narratives were eclipsed by the popularity of *Don Quixote* and of the *Novelas ejemplares* until 1618 when the *Vida del escudero Marcos de Obregón* (*The Life of the Squire Marcos de Obregón*) re-established interest in the genre. Editions of the *Lazarillo* and of the *Guzmán* continued to be printed during this hiatus. Juan de Luna's 'corrected' version of the *Lazarillo* together with his original second part were published in Paris (1620). And a completely new *Lazarillo* was written by Juan Cortes de Tolosa called *El Lazarillo de Manzanares* (Madrid, 1620), portions of which were only slightly modified borrowings from the *Guzmán* and the *Buscón*. There was one exception in this continuing tradition. In 1612 Alonso Jerónimo de Salas Barbadillo published *La hija de Celestina* (*Celestina's Daughter*), a work which many readers have called picaresque. The editor of the Milan 1615 edition offered the novel as an imitation of the *Lazarillo* and the *Guzmán*. He was not making an aesthetic judgement, rather, he merely sought to associate the book with the two most famous *pícaros* in order to sell more copies. Almost from the beginning Elena, the protagonist, travels with Montúfar, the real *pícaro* of the story. After several adventures, during one in which Elena tells Montúfar her life, they end up in Madrid where they are caught and brought to justice. Elena is executed and a third-person narrator provides an epitaph for her grave. *La hija de Celestina* is not a picaresque novel even in a 'loose' sense. The conventions of the autobiographical form, the basic theme of honour and the complex relationships between the *pícaro* and society are absent.

The second phase of the picaresque in Spain begins with Vicente Espinel's *Marcos de Obregón* and includes Jerónimo de Alcalá Yáñez's *Alonso, mozo de muchos amos* (*Alonso, Servant of Many Masters*), First Part, Madrid, 1624, Second Part, Valladolid, 1626, and the anonymous *La vida y hechos de Estebanillo González, hombre de buen humor* (*The Life and Deeds of Estebanillo Gonzalez, a Comedian*), Antwerp, 1646, but published in Spain in 1652 and 1655. Many literary histories describe these works as belonging to the 'agony' or 'tragi-comic' phase of the genre in Spain, picaresque only in a loose sense or even 'anti-picaresque'.

Vicente Espinel's only novel, for instance, shares some elements with its ancestors, notably the first-person narrative, the didactic intent and the episodic structure. However, its differences are perhaps more striking. The most fundamental change is that the 'life' of Marcos is based to a great extent on the biography of Espinel himself. Marcos tells us that he comes from an Old Christian family in Ronda and, although poor, insists on leading an honest life. In this sense *Marcos de Obregón* is an 'anti-picaresque' novel. Even his 'picaresque' tricks are used against other *pícaros*. The urban-centred nature of other novels is replaced with extensive travels. Most of Marcos' career is more reminiscent of a 'Greek' romance than of a picaresque novel. His references to fortune, shipwrecks, imprisonments, 'coincidental' reunions with former friends, disguised young women and strange islands are the stuff of romance. He ends up a squire, not as the result of struggling upward, but by waiting patiently to find his niche in society. Finally, Espinel's narrator has a different attitude towards honour than previous rogues. Like Cervantes before him, Espinel argues that the external honour so sought after by Lazarillo, Guzmán and Pablos – and denied them because of their tainted blood – is illusory and immoral. Being a gentleman should not be based on appearance or race but on a virtuous life.

The author of *Alonso, mozo de muchos amos*, doctor Jerónimo de Alcalá Yáñez y Rivera studied classics and theology at Alcalá and medicine at Valladolid. His religious bent had a particular influence in *Alonso* where, in addition to the overall moral tone of the novel, specific reference is made to the miracle of the Virgin of Fuencisla, a topic to which he devoted a brief pamphlet. The author's medical training and vocation also appear in the novel. One entire chapter exalts the practice of medicine. This sympathetic attitude is a radical departure from other picaresque novels which tend to satirize the medical profession in general and doctors in particular. Yáñez's most important innovation, however, is the use of narrative dialogue as the structuring device of the novel. Alonso is aided in the telling of his own story by a few significant interruptions from his listeners. The total effect of this 'conversational' technique bestows a sense of presence, of 'here and now' to Alonso's past life. Bringing into the book itself the character to whom it is addressed had never been tried before, except, of course, for Cervantes' burlesque version in *The Dogs' Colloquy*.

Alonso relates his life in the first part of the novel to the vicar of the monastery where he is a lay-brother. He begins with his birth and gives an account of the various masters he has served prior to his arrival at the monastery: his uncle, a priest; a group of students, a nobleman in Toledo, a judge in Córdoba, a doctor in Seville, a young widow in Valencia, a constable in Mexico, and a group of actors. Like Marcos before him, Alonso, exhausted by the 'vanities of the world' and seeking refuge from the insecurities of life, retires to the cloister where he hopes to serve and to please only God. He had been there fourteen years before he begins his narration. Alonso has abandoned the monastery in the second part of the book and has become a hermit. He describes his adventures between these events to a parish priest, including details of his experiences with a band of gypsies, his marriage, his service to a Portuguese gentleman, and his many professions. The final episode of his narrated life deals with his imprisonment in Algiers. Ransomed by Trinitarian monks, he returns to Spain where he decides to remain until his death. Alonso's obsessive moralizing defines him more as a preacher than as a *pícaro*, and even from the viewpoint of earlier rogues, he fails to fit the category. His retirement from the world is in one sense an acknowledgement of his 'material' failure, a failure, however, which is overshadowed by 'spiritual' success. Finding inner peace away from society is the lesson learned by Alonso.

The publication in 1646 of *La vida y hechos de Estebanillo González* brings the genre of the Spanish picaresque full circle. Like the *Lazarillo de Tormes* written nearly a century before, the 'life' of Estebanillo was published with the rogue's name on the title page as the 'real' author. He writes his autobiography explicitly in the picaresque tradition but with one fundamental difference, as he explains in the introduction to the reader: 'I want to inform you that it is not like the fictitious one of Guzman de Alfarache, or the legendary one of Lazarillo de Tormes, or even the hypothetical one of the Gentleman of the Pincers [a reference to Quevedo's short satire of the same title, or to the *Buscón* itself], but a true account, with proof and witnesses who are named so that everyone can validate my experiences – where, how and when they took place—.' Estebanillo's life may indeed be the first authentic autobiography of a 'real' *pícaro*.

He dedicates his book to Ottavio Piccolomini, Duke of Amalfi (1599–1656) in whose service Estebanillo spent much of his life. Even though Estebanillo is not employed as Piccolomini's buffoon until chapter seven, the initial episodes recount his early picaresque life: his upbringing in Italy and the adventures which led him to Flanders where he met his famous master. Estebanillo was born in Galicia, Spain, but baptized, he points out, in Rome. And like those rogues of the early picaresque, there is some question about the 'purity' of his ancestors. He reports that his mother, before she died, insisted almost too strongly on their noble blood and on his direct link with the Count Fernán González. Estebanillo's early career follows the pattern of Guzmán's and Pablos'. He too attends school, turns into a practical joker and petty thief and is dismissed and apprenticed to a barber friend of his father. He travels across Europe and witnesses most of the major battles of the Thirty Years War. His journey includes activities reminiscent of earlier *pícaros*. At one point he is called another Lazarillo de Tormes because of the tricks he plays. Elsewhere he exchanges his worn cape for a new one belonging to a Spaniard, echoing a trick Pablos learned from Lorenzo del Pedroso, a fellow thief in Madrid (III, 3).

When Estebanillo accepts a position as professional buffoon to the Duke of Amalfi, he is forced to *act* the role of a *pícaro*, making others laugh but causing himself great discomfort. He remarks how difficult being an 'hombre de buen humor' is when faced daily with horrors such as dismembered bodies, blood, and the general ravages of battles. He admits that he is a coward who would prefer to avoid facing the reality of the world from which there is no escape. War had replaced the conventional 'society' with which previous *pícaros* were forced to contend. Despite the macabre background of Estebanillo's life, his antics, jokes and stories are intended to build a humorous foreground, to entertain his readers and to remind Piccolomini – in a rather grotesque manner – of the necessity for buffoonery in the midst of death. *Estebanillo González*'s foundation lies in the early Spanish picaresque, but its meaning points to the 'present' moment which was defined by the agonizing and enduring political and religious conflicts in seventeenth-century Europe. We will encounter the same theme in Grimmelshausen's *Simplicius Simplicissimus*, another book whose hero and narrator carries on a frustrating search for a tranquil place within the chaos of war.

Estebanillo González takes both the *pícaro* and the picaresque novel in a new direction. No longer is the rogue a penitent criminal (Guzmán) or an obstinate law-breaker (Pablos). Nor does he seek to better himself by associating with 'respectable' people (Lazarillo). Estebanillo's honour, he says at one point, is the pleasure ('gusto') he takes. And he certainly makes no serious claims to a Christian family background (Marcos, Alonso). As a clown he jokes at himself as a rogue and parasite. His solitude, which he shares with his predecessors, defines his status as a comedian. His reference in the final paragraphs to the death of Philip IV's wife (October 6, 1644) does not elicit 'inner' peace, rather it calls forth his depressions and sense of confusion. The clown prepares for his own death, not by doing penitence but by publishing his 'life' in order to entertain and amuse his readers. He remains a clown to the end. The perfectly sustained autobiographical illusion of the *Lazarillo de Tormes* is no longer a literary *tour de force* because it is no longer an illusion. The perfect blending of history and fiction is brought about not by a Renaissance humanist, social reformer or court satirist, but by a clown-author whose words are forced to bear the tragi-comic nature of his life.

3

The picaresque novel in Europe: a literary itinerary of the pícaro

Frank Kearful recently suggested that the 'Spanish picaresque ... is far more validly seen, as a genre, in its own national, historical, formal, thematic, and stylistic contexts than in those of the novel in succeeding centuries in other countries' (p. 383). I am sympathetic to his proposition but at the same time it would be absurd to deny the wholesale exportation of a cluster of picaresque conventions in the light of the numerous 'translations' of Spanish picaresque novels into Italian, German, French and English. I set apart the word 'translations' because they were not translations in the modern sense. The French version of the *Lazarillo*, for instance, carried the title *L'histoire plaisante et facetieuse du Lazare de Tormes espagnol. En laquelle on peult recongnoistre bonne partie des meurs, vie & conditions des espagnolz* (Paris, 1561). Lazarillo's 'fortunas y adversidades' were transformed into an 'amusing history', and a 'joke-book' in which the French reader would learn about the mores, life and condition of Spaniards in general. David Rowland's English translation substituted a different subtitle: *The Pleasaunt Historie of Lazarillo de Tormes a Spaniarde, wherein is conteined his marveilous deeds and life. With the straunge adventures happened to him in the service of sundrie Masters* (London, 1586). Lazarillo's hard life consists of 'straunge adventures', a rather odd way of describing his numerous beatings and near starvation. By the time the *Lazarillo* found its way to Italy, the length of the title had doubled. Barezzo Barezzi offered the public 'con vivaci discorsi, e gratiosi trattenimenti' a wide range of topics: 'ammaestramenti saggi, avenimenti mirabili, capricci curiosi, facetie singolari, sentenze gravi, fatti egregi, detti piacevoli, & proverbi sententiosi' (title page of Venice edition, 1622). Italy, with its strong *liber vagatorum* tradition and vast storehouse of satiric *novelle*, would have found very little that was new in the 'unique' jokes, 'witty' teachings, 'miraculous' events and 'weighty' *sententiae*. The editor of the Milan, 1587 Spanish edition pointed out that the *Lazarillo* had not been selling well. Perhaps, Barezzi thought, it would do better in translation.

The titles were not the only changes made in these translations. When Alemán's *Guzmán de Alfarache* was turned into French by Lesage in 1732, almost half the novel disappeared, along with its meaning, because he decided not to include the digressions – what he called the 'moralités superflues'. And when he translated the 'life' of *Estebanillo González*, he tells us in the 'avant-propos', he filled it with 'plusieurs aventures' taken from *Marcos de Obregón*. Guzmán, Marcos and Estebanillo suffered less than Quevedo's Pablos. In the *Buscón* Pablos courts Doña Ana in order to marry into a respectable family. He is punished for his efforts and hounded out of the Court. In Sieur de la Geneste's translation (Paris, 1633), according to Henry Thomas' description:

> the hero, reaching Seville with a company of players, falls in love with a rich merchant's daughter, . . . named Rozèle. After a course of deceitful wooing, he marries the lady and removes with her to Valladolid to avoid being found out. The lady's father is opportunely drowned in a shipwreck, the news kills her mother . . . , and the now prosperous husband has no difficulty in leading a reformed life. (pp. 284–5)

Sieur de la Geneste gives Pablos what he has sought all along, totally destroying the book's meaning. Much work remains to be done on these 'translations' of Spanish novels throughout Europe. But it is possible to say with some assurance that they are for the most part 'new' works, and a history of them would reveal the gradual 'naturalization' of Spanish picaresque narratives which flourished over several decades.

These translations also served as 'models' for the writing of 'original' fiction. I will look in more detail at a few of the translations, showing how they become 'blends' of the Spanish originals and of already existing 'native' traditions. In some countries Spanish models were easily adaptable to another audience; in others, they hardly made any impact. I will also be concerned in this section with what Ronald Paulson has called the 'mixing of conventions', that is, with the process through which various picaresque 'elements' and 'characteristics' were assimilated, or rejected, by translators and authors.

Italy

Translations of Spanish picaresque novels appeared in Italy slightly later than in other European countries. These translations, however, did not inspire the writing of what could be called an Italian picaresque novel. The *Lazarillo*, as I indicated earlier, was first translated and published by Barezzi in 1622 and was reprinted immediately. E. R. Sims has pointed out that Barezzi's version 'is really a compilation of stories interspersed with moral observations on themes as nobility, honor, love, friendship, ingratitude – all preceded by seven chapters of *sentencias*, quotations from various philosophers – Plato, Socrates, Aristotle and others' (p. 331). It is obvious that Barezzi simply put together a string of his own adaptations of Italian texts, taken mainly from Giraldi Cinthio's *Hecatommithi*, to sell them under the disguise and reputation of Lazarillo, the 'picariglio castigliano'. Barezzi had more success with the *Guzmán*. He translated and published editions in 1606, 1615, 1616, 1621, 1622 and 1629. He also printed his translation of *La pícara Justina* in 1628 and 1629.

Compared to the numerous translations and imitations of the Spanish picaresque in the rest of Europe, these versions seem to have had little impact on Italian literature of the time. Several possible reasons can account for this lack of a continuing tradition. One is that Italy already had a strong history of the kind of *novelle* that Barezzi included in his translations. This native tradition contained tales of trickery and fraud similar to those found in the picaresque, many of which came from the general store of *facetiae* or from other sources such as Theseus Pinus Urbinas' thirteenth-century *De cerretanorum origine eorumque fallaciis*. Italy also had a long tradition of *liber vagatorum* literature. The blind beggar in the *Lazarillo*, Guzmán's fraternity of vagabonds in Rome, Pablos' partner, Valcázar, a false beggar in Madrid, and the hundred odd wandering students and thieves which populated the Spanish picaresque, were commonplace in existing Italian fiction. Rafaele Frianoro's *Il vagabondo, overo sferza de bianti e vagabondi* (1621), Luigi Pulci's lists of 'parole e frasi furbesche', the anonymous *Novo modo de intendere la lingua zerga*, and other anatomies of criminals and beggars, although appearing nearly simultaneously with the first influx of the Spanish picaresque, seem to originate in earlier works or from the 'reality' of the times. Frianoro, for instance, begins his work by referring to the great masses of vagabonds seen everywhere in Italy. His intention is to protect the general populace by revealing the various kinds of false beggars, their language and tricks. In no sense is his book a 'biography' or a novel about an individual tramp.

Germany

Germany too had a strong tradition of literary works which shared characteristics with the Spanish picaresque. The native *Liber vagatorum: Der Betler Orden* with its descriptions and catalogues of false beggars and other social parasites, circulated in manuscript as early as the fourteenth century and was first printed in 1509 or 1510. By 1528 when Martin Luther wrote a Preface for it, more than eighteen editions had been printed. Luther's recension circulated with the title *Von der falschen buebery ... Und hinden auf ein Rotswelsch Vocabularius* (Wittemberg), prominently advertising its third section of beggars' cant. At least thirty-four separate editions of this work were available in the sixteenth and seventeenth centuries, attesting its widespread appeal. In addition to this interest in the lower strata of society in general, German literature also possessed an authentic native 'anti-hero', the *Schalksnarr* ('trickster', 'buffoon'). In the fifteenth-century chapbook, *Till Eulenspiegel*, a stupid and lowly peasant (Eulenspiegel) works his tricks and practical jokes on a 'superior' society. *Eulenspiegel*, however, is not the biography of a rogue, but a stringing together of anecdotes, linguistic puns and clever jests. Some literary historians have claimed that medieval German literature contains an embryonic form of the *Erziehungsroman*, a novel recounting the development and education of a man from ignorance to maturity, in Wolfram von Eschenbach's *Parzival*. As a young man Parzival is referred to as a simple fool, isolated from society, ignorant of worldly ways and lacking in formal, especially religious, education.

The coincidence of these traditions made Germany far more receptive to the Spanish picaresque than was Italy. In 1615 Aegidius Albertinus, sometimes called the 'father' of the German picaresque novel, published an edition of the *Guzmán* in two parts. The first part was a translation of Alemán's first part, enlarged by additions from Martí's spurious sequel. Albertinus composed a new second part which, from the viewpoint of literary history, could be considered the first 'German' picaresque novel. Without having seen the authentic second part, Albertinus unknowingly carried out Alemán's intention to have Guzmán repent. He then promised a third part which was to include Guzmán's pilgrimage to the Holy Land. When this third part finally appeared in 1626, it was written not by Albertinus, but by the pseudonymous Martinus Freudenhold who carried out the original plan, sending Guzmán on his pilgrimage and turning him into a hermit.

The success of these translations illustrates how easily the Spanish picaresque novel was adapted and assimilated into the German fiction of the period. According to some critics, however, the translations of both Albertinus and 'Freudenhold' have little literary merit. This is not the case with Ulenhart's translation of another picaresque text, Cervantes' *Rinconete y Cortadillo*, which is worth reading even today. Ulenhart produced a near 'perfect' version, following the original closely without adding extraneous passages or episodes. He retained the tale's 'realistic' tone by transferring the action from Seville to Prague, by changing the names of the two *pícaros* to German equivalents (Isaak Winterfelder and Jobst von der Schneid) and adding a few years to their ages, and finally, by replacing Spanish thieves' cant (*germanía*) with German *Rotwelsch*. Even the drink preferred by thieves is transformed. In Seville they drink wine; in Prague thieves order beer. Ulenhart prized his version of Cervantes' text so highly that he published it under his own name.

In the seventeenth century the native German traditions found new expression in the work of Hans Jacob Christoffel von Grimmelshausen (1621?–1676). In 1668 Grimmelshausen published *The Adventurous Simplicissimus, or the True Description of the Life of a Strange Vagabond, named Melchior Sternfels von Fuchshaim.* It was followed by a *Continuatio* in 1669. A year later *The Life Story of the Arch-Swindler and Runagate Courage* was published, reflecting Grimmelshausen's continuing interest in rogue fiction. Even though Albertinus was one of Grimmelshausen's favourite authors, there is no conclusive evidence to prove that he knew either Albertinus' or Freudenhold's versions of the *Guzmán*. Grimmelshausen did use Albertinus' 1604 translation of Antonio de Guevara's *Menosprecio de corte y alabanza de aldea* (Valladolid, 1539), a work which praises country life over the corrupt life at the Court. As R. O. Jones describes it, 'life in the village is more comfortable and healthy, food is cheaper and better, a man is not surrounded by flatterers and scandalmongers' (p. 20). With slight modifications Grimmelshausen quotes several passages from Albertinus' translation of Guevara at the end of *Simplicissimus* just before the narrator leaves 'this world' for the 'lonely woods'.

The so-called 'Simplician' writings include the five-book 1668 text as well as a series of five sequels. We will consider only the 1668 text which is a 'complete' novel in itself. Like the Spanish *pícaros* before him, Simplicissimus begins the narrative with his birth and early years. On the surface he is similar to Honofre in that he comes from 'peasant' stock. The walls of his father's house are hung with 'fine tapestries', that is, cobwebs. And like Lázaro he focuses on the opposition between honour bestowed by one's noble ancestry and the honour that is 'earned', in this case, that is bought with money and fine clothes: '... by nature I am inclined toward the business of nobility, if only I had the necessary tools and investment capital for it' (p. 3). Only at the end of the novel does he discover that a hermit he has met is his 'real' father, a nobleman who gave up the 'world' to retire to the forest. Simplicissimus is as 'simple' as his name indicates. Reflecting back on the early part of his life, he writes: 'I was so perfect and excellent in ignorance that I could not possibly have known that I knew nothing at all' (p. 5). He is described with the same words applied to Parzival, a 'reiner Tor' ('simpleton'), and as befits his intellectual level, he begins his career as a 'herdsman'.

Simplicissimus' pastoral world is destroyed when soldiers burn his home, abduct his family, and leave him for dead. From this point on he is condemned to a picaresque life played out, like Estebanillo's, against the backdrop of the Thirty Years War. He wanders across Europe, serving several masters and develops a worldly sophistication amid the horrors of war. By the end of the second book, his reputation as a thief and trickster is well established. At the height of his career, like Quevedo's Pablos, he lies awake at night planning new strategies: 'I was so eager for honour and glory that I could hardly sleep, and when I lay awake many a night thinking up new tricks...' (p. 132). After many careers – buffoon, soldier, male prostitute, 'doctor' and pilgrim – he returns to his native soil as the Treaty of Westphalia is being signed (1648). As peace returns to Germany, he takes account of his life and seeks the tranquillity of retreat. But there is one final irony:

> I would have liked to live near my mineral spring, but the peasants of the neighborhood did not want me, though the lonely woods suited me well. They feared that I might give away the secret of the spring and get their lord to build trails and a road to it, now that peace had come. Therefore, I went to another wild place and resumed the life I had led in the Spessart. (p. 329)

He can not return 'home' because he is no longer 'simple'. Unlike the Spanish *pícaros* who attempt to escape their pasts and especially the identifying marks of their homes, Simplicissimus makes a futile effort to shed his past infamous life by returning to his neighbourhood. The innocence and simplicity of Nature would have been violated had he been successful. His experiences are seen as a contaminator of the pure 'mineral spring'. On another level Grimmelshausen seems to be saying that thirty years of war have left precious little to which the participants are able to return. The smells, sights and general degradation of violent death and destruction are inescapable. The 'dignity of man', then, is seen in *Simplicissimus* as a fragile veneer, which is worth saving, however, because the alternatives are far worse.

Simplicissimus grows to self-knowledge and to human dignity. On his pilgrimage in the fifth book, he has sincerely repented of his 'vicious and godless' life: 'Then and there I publicly embraced the Catholic faith, went to confession, and after absolution partook of the Eucharist' (p. 267). His repentance implies that he could have chosen to live otherwise, although within the world of the novel, his only real choice was to be the victim or the victimizer. His effort to control his own destiny in the midst of war is frustrated throughout the book. He is the plaything of random violence. In Simplicissimus' case Grimmelshausen injects grace, the possibility of penitence and salvation. The Heartbrothers and his hermit father seem to be the only virtuous characters he meets. And it is primarily through them that he begins to evaluate his wasted past.

There is one fundamental difference between Simplicissimus and the Spanish *pícaro*. German rogues have 'noble' blood. Simplicissimus' father was Captain Sternfels von Fuchshaim; Courage's father, a count who fled to Turkey. Both of Grimmelshausen's rogues begin their lives with the possibility of improving themselves, but war destroys their 'birthright', turning them into failures. *Simplicissimus* follows Alemán's version of the picaresque by repenting at the end. *Courage* follows the pattern of the *Buscón* in which the *pícaro* is disillusioned but remains an obstinate sinner. Grimmelshausen captures the basic 'instability' of the rogue's open-ended life by preventing his characters from escaping war. Only when peace treaties are signed do they have the opportunity to settle in one place. But, as we have seen, Simplicissimus is forced to move from his homeland, while Courage, as a gypsy, has no homeland at all. Nearly all their 'masters' are related to one degree or another to the business of war. War, then, is their ultimate master. Never able to escape it, nor to profit by it permanently, their lives, even though punctuated frequently with tricks, jokes and laughter, consist of fragmented experiences which they attempt to put together through their autobiographies. Finally, both of Grimmelshausen's rogues are degenerative parasites who are even unable to reproduce themselves. Like their Spanish predecessors, they have no children. It may be accidental but Grimmelshausen's novels generated no similarly famous narratives in Germany.

France

Translations of Spanish picaresque novels appeared in France earlier and in greater quantity than anywhere in Europe. The *Lazarillo*, first translated in 1560, circulated in five different versions by 1678. The first part of the *Guzmán* was read in French the year after the Spanish original was published in Madrid. Altogether there were four distinct versions of the *Guzmán*, the final one being the translation of Lesage in 1732. All were reprinted several times. *Marcos de Obregón* had a French audience the same year it was being read in Madrid. *La pícara Justina* as *La Narquoise* ['Cunning'] *Justine* was available in 1635, following Sieur de la Geneste's translation of the *Buscón* by two years. Quevedo's work was clearly one of the most popular novels, la Geneste's version being reprinted at least twenty times. Finally, Cervantes' *Novelas ejemplares*, containing several *pícaros* and picaresque stories, were turned into French in 1615.

The *liber vagatorum* tradition and criminal biographies and vocabularies, already well established in France, gained momentum with the sudden importation of Spanish picaresque novels. The *Avertissement, antidote et remède contre les piperies des pipeurs* (Paris, 1584) contained the biography of Antoine d'Anthenay, a notorious criminal of the time. In 1596 *La vie généreuse des Mercelots, Gueux et Bohémiens, contenant leur façon de vivre, subtilité et gergon* appeared in Lyon, but only became a best-seller after being 'introduced' by the Spanish picaresque. It was reprinted in Paris in 1612, 1618, 1621 and 1622. 'Pechon de Ruby', the author, joins a group of beggars, learns their language and tricks and finally leaves them to roam with some gypsies who teach him the art of necromancy. A list of thieves' vocabulary concludes the book. Dr Carlos García, a Spanish teacher residing in Paris, published *La desordenada codicia de los bienes ajenos* in 1619. Dr García's book is one of the most detailed and complete catalogues of thieves ever written. These publications, together with the translations of Spanish picaresque novels, supplied new and interesting 'facts' to those readers who were curious about the lives and experiences of criminals and beggars. Contemporary historical events stimulated a wider popular interest in the subject. While historians remain uncertain whether more crimes were committed after the turn of the century than before, municipal and royal authorities and the general public – as in England – became more concerned about 'law and order'. Duelling, for instance, though not an activity associated with vagrants and common thieves, became an 'official' crime subject to prosecution. In an atmosphere of heightened awareness of crime, what better way was there to learn about criminality than by reading the life of the *gueux* Guzmán who was sentenced to the galleys?

The picaresque novel was 'read' in other ways too. Its so-called realism and satiric tone agreed perfectly with the attitudes of writers such as Sorel and Scarron who were reorienting literary tastes away from idealized romances towards contemporary matters. Charles Sorel (1602–1674) and Paul Scarron (1610–1660) were two of the earliest French satirists to exploit the picaresque. The *pícaro* was an 'anti-hero' who satirized and victimized a corrupt society. Even though *Don Quixote* was the model for most anti-romances and realistic fiction, picaresque novels were rifled for material and satiric technique.

Antoine Adam correctly points out, however, that what distinguishes a character like Francion from *pícaros* are his lineage and birth. He is a 'gentilhomme', proud of his nobility and of the true values of the *noblesse*. His exposure of false gentlemen and of ignorant courtiers who masquerade as true noblemen echoes the satiric vision of a Quevedo. Like Marcos de Obregón before him – who in the same sense is not a *pícaro* – he observes the rogues around him and *acts* as one in order to present an 'authentic' account of social corruption. Even though he may be caught up in the ricocheting effect of his own satire, he nevertheless stands apart from the punishment he heaps on others. Thus in the process of attacking only a corrupt and pretentious society, Sorel and Scarron lost the sense of the picaresque novel. Their 'heroes' are no longer *pícaros* but *gentilhommes* who want to be more than they are in fact. They are not born dishonourably into poverty, but into a 'bourgeois' society as defined by Furetière and Molière, and their wit, tricks, disguises and stories are employed to chastize their own society. Neither is there any concern with the relationships between their past experiences and 'present' situations. Their roles as authors of their own lives are subordinated to the outward direction of their satire. They are presented as full-grown, experienced satirists and comedians whose 'innocence' is soon lost after they enter the novels.

The generic patterns established by the picaresque novel survive in France almost exclusively in their 'translations', and even then with sometimes radical modifications. Doubtless there were exceptions such as Tristan l'Hermite's *Page disgracié* (1642), seen as picaresque because of its autobiographical point of view, but they are rare. Picaresque novels in France became comic narratives and as such, had to be 'cleansed' of many of the elements which made them picaresque in the first place. Quevedo's condemnation of his rogue Pablos to a life of frustration and failure after a career of pranks and jokes is not a comic ending. Sieur de la Geneste's transformation of Pablos into a 'reformed' rogue is simply another way of seeing him as a successful comedian. The 'French' Pablos has the last laugh. Lesage goes beyond the elimination of digressions and moral commentary in his translation of the *Guzmán* by releasing him from the galleys and making him promise to live 'une vie plus raisonnable'. A. A. Parker has stated that these translations 'are historically of cardinal importance since they are the bridge between Alemán and Lesage and can alone explain the changes that the picaresque tradition underwent as it moved into the eighteenth century' (p. 111). He is correct with the exception of those picaresque echoes, themes and conventions which blended into other fictional forms in seventeenth-century France. Lesage's 'original' fiction, however, is the best example of this intermixing of conventions.

Alain René Lesage (1668–1747) wrote and published the *Histoire de Gil Blas de Santillane* over several years. Volumes I and II appeared in 1715, III in 1724 (in an 'Edition nouvelle') and IV in 1735. *Gil Blas* is a novel in the tradition of the French 'translations' of Spanish picaresque novels. His intention is 'representer la vie des hommes telle qu'elle est' ('to portray the life of men as it really is'), not in France, but in Spain. Gil Blas' travels, however, are no more Spanish than Montesquieu's *Lettres persanes* are Persian or Antoine Bret's *La belle Allemande* is German. Even within his 'Spanish' atmosphere Gil Blas is not a Spanish *pícaro*. He tells us in the first chapter that his father was a retired soldier and his mother a 'petite bourgeoise', adding that he was (properly) born ten months after their marriage. His parents moved to Valladolid to find work and left Gil Blas in the care of his priest uncle to obtain a good education. His uncle, however, is so uneducated that he is unable to teach his pupil the rudiments of Latin. Gil ridicules him, not because he is the miserly and miserable priest of the *Lazarillo* or Pablos' avaricious teacher in the *Buscón*, but because he is the most ignorant ecclesiastic in his order. His only fault, then, is his lack of education. We are clearly in the eighteenth century.

From the beginning of the novel it is obvious that we are not reading another *Lazarillo*, *Guzmán* or *Buscón*. Gil Blas' preface to the reader, his description of his birth, parents and uncle, and his intention to attend the University of Salamanca, identifies Lesage's direct contact with the Spanish picaresque to its later development, specifically to the first 'anti-picaresque' novel, the *Marcos de Obregón*. As Parker puts it, 'roguery exists not in him but in the world outside him' (p. 121). Soon after he leaves home he is robbed, tricked into selling his mule, captured by a gang of robbers and taken to an underground dwelling very reminiscent of Monipodio's house in *Rinconete y Cortadillo*. Even though he commits a robbery, a life of crime is not to his liking. As soon as he escapes he creates for himself more comfortable surroundings by dressing and acting like a gentleman. He later becomes an apprentice, not a servant, to one Dr Sangrado (the French metamorphosis of Dr Sagredo in *Marcos de Obregón*) and elevates himself quickly to the position of a prospering doctor in Valladolid.

Gil Blas' 'life' consists in the narration of his adventures with various masters and the life-stories they tell him while he is in their service. This device allows him to cover all levels of society, from bandits (Don Raphael) to aristocrats (Count Duke of 'Olivarez'). He reaches the high point of his career when he masquerades as an aristocrat himself. This forces him to hide his 'bourgeois' origins, to deny his 'blood': 'In a word, my pride and vanity had swelled to such a height, that my father and mother were no longer among the number of my honored relatives. Alas! poor understrappers, I never thought of asking whether you had sunk or were swimming in the Asturias. A thought about you never came into my head. The

court has all the soporific virtues of Lethe in the case of poor relations' (III, 52). He is made aware in a very physical way to what
extent the 'Court' can corrupt when he is cast into prison for
certain 'courtly' activities, namely escorting the prince of Spain to a
house of 'suspicious' character. His lesson is reinforced when he
nearly dies from a fever. Still in prison he decides to change his
'inner' life, to reform himself:

> I looked at wealth and honors with the eye of a dying anchorite,
> and blessed the malady which restored my soul. I abjured courts,
> politics, and the Duke of Lerma. If ever my prison doors were
> opened, it was my fixed resolve to buy a cottage, and live like a
> philosopher. (III, 109)

The rest of his 'biography' consists of several journeys during
which he is reunited with old friends – Scipio, his servant,
Fabricio and Dr Sangrado – meeting them in the contexts of
historical events such as the Revolution in Portugal and the 'fall' and
death of Olivarez. Like Marcos before him, he returns home older
and wiser, not for the purpose of writing his memoirs, but to
marry. No longer 'middle class', he settles down in his castle at
Lirias to lead a life of 'unmixed bliss in this beloved society. To
perfect my satisfaction, heaven has deigned to send me two smiling
babies, whose education will be the amusement of my declining
years; and if ever a husband might venture to hazard so bold an
hypothesis, I devoutly believe myself their father' (III, 407).

I have, of course, stressed the serious picaresque aspects of Gil
Blas' life, not mentioning his many tricks, love-affairs, travels with
actors and actresses, and his involvement in questionable
activities. The fact is that he never really becomes a *pícaro* in the
Spanish sense. He is rarely if ever on the verge of starvation nor is he
an obsessive thief or gambler. Money seems not to be a problem.
Moreover his role as a satirist of morals and manners, especially
of political intrigue, favouritism and bribery, demands that he
participate but only to show how 'wrong' they are. Spanish-type
pícaros are present in the novel but not in the figure of Gil Blas.
As Werner Bahner has indicated, Gil Blas rejects the criminal-
picaresque careers of Raphael and Ambrose. Their lives are put in
the context of the lives of characters from other social strata and

are offered as one possibility that Gil Blas can pursue. He senses, however, that they lead 'downward' when in effect his background and goals point in the other direction. Even his name augurs a socially high position. Iñigo López de Mendoza was made Marquis of the town of Santillana in the fifteenth century. His descendants were members of the highest and most respected Spanish nobility. While most Spanish *pícaros* chose illustrious names to hide their dishonourable ancestry, Lesage uses it to locate his narrator's final 'happy' position within his 'Spanish' society. The son of a soldier and a 'petite bourgeoise' is ennobled through his experiences. In another sense he simply becomes his name.

Gil Blas, written in the tradition of the 'anti-picaresque' novel, is a narrative of 'actions comiques' which contain, if we are able to believe the narrator, some serious reflections of a little philosopher. The light comedy of the novel in comparison with the 'serious' tone of Spanish picaresque novels may be the reason why Parker views *Gil Blas* as a trivial book in the context of its ancestors. His interpretation, however, might be contrasted with that of Felix Brun who has said that 'it is the perspective of victorious individualism, made possible by the new social base that the French bourgeoisie of the eighteenth century offered which is the essential characteristic of *Gil Blas* (cited by Bahner, p. 10). From the viewpoint of the picaresque tradition, Lesage has managed to adapt virtually every convention of the genre in his creation of an 'anti-picaresque' work. His radical transformation of both rogue and society allow Gil Blas to find success and stability in a country setting. His convenient marriage symbolizes a 'new' society in which, at least in fiction, class distinctions no longer exist.

England

The history of the picaresque novel in England follows to some degree its development in France. An early translation of the *Lazarillo* by David Rowland (1568) was not published until 1576. The second edition of 1586, the earliest extant text, gives a clear idea of how Rowland interpreted the interests of his English audience. In the preface he describes the contents of his translation as 'strange and mery reports, very recreative & pleasant', whose readers could look forward to 'a true description of the nature & disposition of sundrie Spaniards. So that by reading hereof, such as have not travailed Spaine, may as well discerne much of the maners & customs of that countrey, as those that have there long time continued' (cited from D. B. J. Randall, pp. 58–9). The *Lazarillo* was a 'Spanish' work even in English, both a 'comic' and 'travel' book. William Phiston translated the 1555 sequel in 1596. While Phiston's version seems not to have been reissued, Rowland's *Lazarillo* was reprinted in 1596, 1624, and 1653.

Lazarillo's experience with the blind beggar, especially, tended to associate the novel with the strong native *liber vagatorum* and anatomy of roguery traditions. Robert Copland's *Hye Way to the Spyttel House* (1535), John Awdeley's *Fraternitye of Vagabonds* (1561), Thomas Harmon's *A Caveat or Warening for Common Cursetors Vulgarely called Vagabonds* (1566) and Robert Greene's *Black Bookes Messenger* (1592) attest to the presence of an experienced reading public and enterprising book publishers throughout the sixteenth century. Randall further points out that Andrew Borde's *Geystes of Skoggon* (1565) 'was the first English book to be based on the exploits of a single knave-hero' (p. 67). Thomas Nashe's *The Unfortunate Traveller or the Life of Jack Wilton* (1594) is another example of this relatively well developed pseudo-biographical tradition. In spite of Fredson Bowers' insistence that Nashe was 'modifying and developing' the *Lazarillo* 'according to the English temper and his own inclinations' (p. 26), it contains little of the basic design or theme of the Spanish picaresque. I cite only one example. The servant–master relationship in the *Lazarillo* is almost completely absent from Nashe's book: 'Jack Wilton, though a servant of the Earl of Surrey, is most of the time virtually an independent agent' (Paulson, p. 42).

These 'native' traditions were reinforced with Mabbe's translation of the *Guzmán de Alfarache*. James Mabbe (1572–1642?) published his translation, *The Rogue or the Life of Guzman de Alfarache*, in 1622, and following the lead of its Spanish original, it became an immediate best-seller. It was reissued in 1622, 1623, 1630, 1633, 1634, 1655 and 1656. In reference to its quality, Ben Jonson wrote that it contained 'the noblest marke of a good Booke'.

The first part was translated directly from Spanish; the second part seems to have been based partly on Barezzi's Italian version. Its impact is somewhat difficult to assess. However, during the second half of the century several other books advertise Guzmán's presence in their titles if not in their content. Although *Sonne of the Rogue* (1638) followed close on the heels of its 'father', it was actually a translation of Dr García's *Desordenada codicia de los bienes ajenos*. In 1657 it was retitled *Guzman, Hind and Hannam Outstript*. George Fidge's *English Gusman* (1652), Richard Head's and Francis Kirkman's *The English Rogue Described in the Life of Meriton Latroon* (1665 [Head], 1668 [Kirkman], 1671 [together]), and the anonymously translated *The French Rogue* (1672), *The Dutch Rogue, or Guzman of Amsterdam*, as well as other titles too numerous to mention, all establish a clear strain of 'English' picaresque based partly on Alemán's novel. Several other Spanish picaresque texts also appeared in the second half of the seventeenth century. Salas Barbadillo's *La hija de Celestina* was translated via Scarron's French version by John Davies of Kidwelly in 1657. Davies also translated the *Buscón* from Sieur de la Geneste's loose version.

It is important to recognize that in England even within the seventeenth century several authors distinguished between English 'rogues' and Spanish *pícaros*. The anonymous *Don Tomaso, or the Juvenile Rambles of Thomas Dangerfield* (1680) contains a passage which refers to the 'difference between a Spanish and an English Guzman, the one pursuing a poor hungry plot upon his penurious master's bread and cheese, the other designing to grasp the riches of the fourth part of the world by the ruin of the national commerce', that is, taking over 'the whole Guinea trade' (cited by Paulson, p. 42). It is the 'mercantile' interests of the 'English Guzman' which set him apart from his Spanish predecessor. Molho concisely states the Spanish viewpoint: 'In picaresque thought, anti-honour is identified with money and merchandizing...' (p. cxxv). Because he operated within an hierarchical society in which honour and status were defined by birth and lineage, by 'blood', the Spanish *pícaro* had no recourse to commerce as a means of achieving his goals.

While Defoe seems to have sensed the existence of these basic societal differences, his fiction none the less has a basic similarity to the Spanish picaresque. In Paulson's words 'he wanted to show what it is like to struggle for survival in a marginal situation' (p. 44). Defoe lived a marginal existence most of his adult life. Like Alemán, he too was a failure as a tradesman, dying in straitened circumstances in Ropebaker's Alley in 1731. He was an 'isolated and solitary figure in his time', Ian Watt tells us, who sketched a brief autobiography in one of his pamphlets: 'how I stand alone in the world, abandoned by those very people that own I have done them service; ... how with ... no helps but my own industry, I have forced misfortune, and reduced them [debts], exclusive of composition, from seventeen to less than five thousand pounds; how, in gaols, in retreats, in all manner of extremities, I have supported myself without the assistance of friends or relations' (Watt, p. 90). Defoe was conscious of 'social' as well as 'economic' isolation. In a very interesting treatise from our point of view, *The Compleat English Gentleman*, written towards the end of his life but not published until 1890, he approaches Lázaro's complaint regarding those who inherit 'noble' estates because of their lineage as opposed to those who earn their status as gentlemen through hard work:

> As those gentlemen who have thus descended to commerce claim a rank, as abov [*sic*], by blood, so those rais'd meerly by the help of fortune claim the same advantage with the help of time; that is to say, the merchant or the trades-men whose application thus bless't has lay'd the foundacion of a family in his accumulated wealth, as he seldome arrives to the hight, till he is, as we say, advanc't in years, so the race as gentlemen seldome begin with him. He may be call'd the founder of the family, but his posterity are the gentlemen.... (p. 267)

Defoe indicates that honour is attainable by handling the goods of others, an idea Lázaro expresses *ironically* at the end of his career as he profits from his manipulation of the Archpriest's whore and wine. The Spanish *pícaro* has no such recourse to mercantile pursuits, as we have said, because he has been condemned by his blood.

Defoe's *The Fortunes and Misfortunes of the Famous Moll*

Flanders, published in 1722, is the 'success' story of a female rogue. Moll was born in 'Newgate, and during a life of continu'd variety for threescore years, besides her childhood, was twelve year a whore, five times a wife (whereof once to her own brother), twelve year a thief, eight year a transported felon in Virginia, at last grew rich, liv'd honest and died a penitent' (subtitle). Prosperity and penitence go hand in hand and, apparently, in that order. It seems on the surface as if crime pays. But the nature of crime itself is redefined in *Moll Flanders*. For Moll it is more 'criminal' to be poor and insecure than to be a criminal in the ordinary sense. Thus in a rather paradoxical way the crimes she commits in the novel reflect her efforts not to be a 'criminal', not to find herself in Newgate. From the beginning her goal is to be a 'gentlewoman', that is 'one that did not go to service, to do housework' (p. 10). She wants to be self-sufficient, to be her own 'economic' system as it were. Her early references to making things with her hands to sell define a strong 'inner' desire to affirm control over her destiny. Instead she becomes a 'servant to many masters', mainly to men, subject to their manipulation and control. She discovers that selling her 'favours' – as a whore, wife or mistress – produces hard cash and comfort. Social and sexual morality are commodities to be bought and sold. In this sense Moll becomes an 'economist' of the first order. The orthodox concepts of good and evil are, as in Lázaro's world, subject to Moll's profit and pleasure.

From the moment that Moll understands 'life' as a mercantile venture until she is thrown into prison for having gone too 'often to the well', she has sold her virginity, been married, found good fortune as a mistress, given birth to several children and become a common pickpocket and thief. She is given the death-sentence for 'robbery and house-breaking, that is, for felony and burglary' (p. 315). While in prison she meets one of her former husbands, and instead of being executed, she is 'transported' with him to Virginia to work out her sentence as a convicted criminal. Fortunately she takes her criminally acquired wealth, investing carefully to become a rich planter. And after searching out and finding her son (by her brother-husband), she reconciles his incestuous birth with her own dishonourable past: they have all obtained 'gentility', security and wealth. She returns to England, is later joined by her husband, in 'good heart and health' (p. 384), and both resolve to spend the rest of their lifes in 'sincere penitence' (*ibid.*).

Despite Robert Alter's remark that it is 'more misleading than instructive to call *Moll Flanders* a picaresque novel', Defoe's fiction reveals some of the concerns and conventions of his Spanish predecessors, especially of the *Lazarillo* and the *Guzmán*. Moll's definition of morality in terms of her changing situations, her association of poverty and criminality, her desire for upward mobility and her status as an 'outsider' in a society whose value system is based on wealth and costume, echo some of the basic themes of the early Spanish picaresque. In reality, however, Defoe's so-called picaresque fiction derives from another tradition as John Richetti and others have demonstrated. The first-person narrative viewpoint, the concentrated interest on crime, crime reporting and courts of law are all part of the conventional elements of criminal biographies of the period. The *pícaro*'s pranks and petty thievery are replaced with serious felonies. Finally the 'successful' conclusions to the careers of Defoe's criminals are absent in Spanish picaresque novels. Moll is not a failed 'outsider'; she manages to overcome misfortune and adverse circumstances through determination, ingenuity and hard work.

As we have seen, the criminal strain of the Spanish picaresque merged with already existing European *liber vagatorum*, criminal biography and anatomy of roguery traditions. These European rogues, however, often rose above their disreputable backgrounds and poverty to occupy a higher social status. Even though some of them were unaware of their 'advantages' at the beginning, they usually discovered their 'middle-class' or 'noble' ancestry. At the end of their lives, far from being hunted fugitives or social outcasts, they had improved their situations considerably. Whether country gentlemen, prosperous planters or pilgrim-hermits, they had advanced beyond the level of mere survival.

Such is the case with the hero of *The Adventures of Roderick Random*, Smollett's first novel published in 1748. Tobias George Smollett (1721–1771) translated Lesage's *Gil Blas* in 1749, and he tells us in the Preface to *Roderick Random* that his own novel was consciously based on Lesage's narrative. Even though Lesage disguised his novel as a 'Spanish' work, Smollett recognized the 'illusion' and disapproved of it: 'The following sheets I have modelled on his plan, taking the liberty, however, to differ from him in execution, where I thought his particular situations were uncommon, extravagant, or peculiar to the country in which the scene is laid' (p. xvii). By 'plan' Smollett meant *Gil Blas*' episodic structure and first-person narrator: 'I have attempted to represent modest merit struggling with every difficulty to which a friendless orphan is exposed, from his own want of experience, as well as from the selfishness, envy, malice, and base indifference of mankind' (p. xvii). Paulson concisely describes Smollet's purpose: 'He explains the convention of the inexperienced orphan-outcast hero as providing an object so alone and exploitable as to bring out the best and worst in the people encountered along the road' (p. 167). Roderick is more an English 'foundling' than a Spanish *pícaro*. This is especially apparent when Smollett decides to give him 'the advantages of birth and education', one of the principal reasons being that Roderick is thus able to reassume his 'high' position at the end of the novel by simply finding out who he is.

Roderick's 'random' career begins much the same way, except of course for his birth, as some of his Spanish and French predecessors. He is sent to school, is insulted by another student because of his poverty, and avenges the insult by breaking the student's head with a board. The insult and subsequent physical violence are reminiscent of Pablos' early school days in the *Buscón*, but all similarities end at this point. Roderick does well in school, learning classical languages and studying literature (like Marcos and Gil Blas), and advancing himself in the eyes of others. He too has an uncle (like Pablos), a Mr Bowling, who is a sea man, not a town executioner. Roderick also is an assistant to an apothecary, but he is never a 'servant of many masters'. Instead, he has his own servant, Strap, a former schoolmate, who provides their necessities. Roderick's 'life' is thus confined and servile to his own needs. He 'is only vaguely concerned with the problem of survival or security; rather, he seeks adventure for its own sake, a circumstance which allows Smollett a larger range for his satire than was available to his models' (Paulson, p. 168).

Roderick's adventures are far-flung indeed. He and Strap travel to London where Roderick is assaulted by a press-gang and ends up in irons on a 'man-of-war' called *Thunder*. A long sea voyage ensues during which he visits Jamaica, Hispaniola and Carthagena. Roderick contracts 'distemper', is cured and made a surgeon's mate on another sloop of war. He finally returns to Europe, meets and falls in love with Narcissa, his future bride. After taking part in a duel, among other adventures, he is arrested for an outstanding debt to his tailor. He is released and sails again, this time to South America, where he becomes involved in the slave trade. Making his way to Argentina, he meets a rich gentleman, Don Rodrigo, who turns out to be his long absent father. They both return to England where Roderick rejoins Narcissa. His father regains the family estate, supplying Roderick a 'home' to which he can retire: 'If there be such a thing as true happiness on earth I enjoy it. The impetuous transports of my passion are now settled and mellowed into endearing fondness and tranquillity of love, rooted by that intimate connexion and interchange of hearts which nought but virtuous wedlock can produce' (p. 468). And echoing the 'happy-ending' of *Gil Blas*, Roderick is looking forward to being a father 'to crown my felicity' (*ibid*.).

From almost every viewpoint *Roderick Random* is an example of the already distintegrated picaresque novel. Smollett does salvage a few of the conventions, but even they are redefined within the context of his satiric aims. At first glance he seems to retain the narrator as an 'orphan' attempting to contend with a repressive, corrupt society, but he undercuts this element by having him reunite with his father, thus establishing a 'family' continuity absent from the picaresque novel. He employs the first-person narrative but uses it in a different manner. The 'I' is the consistent voice of a satirist, lashing out at everything that enters his vision. Roderick satirizes others but is rarely the object of ridicule or satire. He is not like Pablos who, although a satirist in his own right, is also a victim of Quevedo's satiric barbs. Roderick is thus 'not a fool (to some knavish master) or a passive touchstone but a satiric observer who recognizes, reacts, and rebukes' (Paulson, p. 171). Finally Smollett fills his novel with what resembles the violence and cruelty so characteristic of the Spanish picaresque. But instead it is the staple material of classical satire, 'particularly as practiced by the Elizabethan imitators of Juvenal and Persius' (Paulson, p. 172) and not the physical picaresque 'servant-master' confrontations. The romance-like plot of *Roderick Random* can scarcely hold together the impassioned and frantic movement of Smollett's satire. Roderick embodies this ricocheting movement in his expression of protest at 'the base indifference of mankind'.

Much closer to the Spanish picaresque in theme and tone is Smollett's *The Adventures of Ferdinand Count Fathom* (1753), described by A. A. Parker as the only eighteenth-century English novel 'that is fully picaresque ... directly in the tradition started by *Guzmán de Alfarache*' (p. 127), despite the fact that it is not even written in the autobiographical form. There is no doubt that Smollett was conscious of the Spanish picaresque tradition. In the first chapter he refers to those readers 'who delight in following Guzman d'Alfarache, through all the mazes of squalid beggery' (I, 8). Ferdinand, however, is a criminal throughout the novel. He finally ends up in prison where he abruptly repents, beginning a new life in a country house. Ferdinand's marriage to Elinor at the end of the novel – the 'happy ending' – points more towards Lesage's version of the picaresque than towards the novelists in the Spanish tradition. However, Ferdinand's extensive travels (England, Austria, France and Germany), his clever thefts and deceptions and the efforts of several characters in the novel to engage in the most venal activities to sustain their 'honour' are more than superficial echoes of the picaresque. In spite of a clear development of Fathom's criminal career which would lead him to the gallows or at least to being 'transported' in the manner of Moll Flanders, Smollett for some reason can not resist a 'Lesage' ending. It is somehow more acceptable for Smollett to sacrifice literary verisimilitude than to punish his narrator.

The picaresque: genre and myth

The idea of the picaresque that emerges out of our brief sixteenth-through eighteenth-century European itinerary is based on a group of novels conceived and written within conventions established by Spanish narratives. We can summarize more specifically: (1) The picaresque novel *sensu strictu* comprises a few Spanish works closely associated with the *Lazarillo de Tormes* and the *Guzmán de Alfarache*. (2) The 'translations' of these novels were largely adaptations which feature the formal elements of the genre (narrative point of view, episodic structure, satiric purpose and the 'servant-master' relationship). (3) The 'imitations' tended to be blends of the adaptations and 'native' fiction and sensibilities. (4) As a result the *pícaro* became or was replaced with the English 'rogue' and 'foundling', the Italian 'vagabundo', the German 'Schelm' and the French 'gueux' or 'gentilhomme'. (5) Finally, his 'picaresque' adventures and level in society were made to conform to the peculiar satiric, social and historical contexts of each country, the general effect of which was to turn him into an 'anti-*pícaro*'.

The *pícaro* himself was perhaps the most radically changed element of the genre. He began as the dishonourable offspring of thieves and prostitutes. His parents were descended from questionable ancestry, often from *conversos*. He was generally required to abandon home at an early age because of poverty and hunger in order to improve his situation. His goal was to serve himself, although he ended up serving others, and eventually to associate with people of means and honour. His knowledge of right and wrong was acquired through his experiences in the world, and invariably it was defined in terms of his own profit. The second phase of the picaresque in Spain reveals a modification of all these characteristics. The narrator was more an adventurer than a rogue. He was born of more respectable parents. Thus his dishonourable beginnings were no longer an issue. His involvement in crime was often an effort on the part of the 'real' author to disclose the crimes and corruption of those with whom he came in contact. At the end of his career he repented of his evil ways and prepared to die. The final novel in the Spanish tradition brought the genre full circle in one sense by recalling the early *pícaro*, but only to point him in another direction by transforming him into a self-conscious clown.

The translations of Spanish picaresque novels are the key to an understanding of the European history of the genre. Translators were 'readers' who not only injected their own tastes and attitudes in their translations, but also assessed and attempted to include the sensibilities of a wider 'invisible' reading public. Their motivations were financial, political and social in nature despite the fact that many of them presented their work to the public as entertainment or edification. In Italy Barezzi virtually monopolized the genre, and although he tended to follow the original texts with some degree of accuracy, he completely changed their emphasis and contexts by adding extraneous material, usually drawn from Italian *novelle* and Renaissance philosophers and moralists. In Germany Albertinus translated more loosely, adding material not in Alemán's original. Without access to the authentic second part, he unwittingly carried out Alemán's project apparently as a result of his Counter-Reformation attitudes. And while it is possible that Grimmelshausen was familiar with Albertinus' translation and perhaps Freudenhold's continuation, there is no firm evidence that he had them in mind or in front of him when he prepared to write *Simplicissimus*. Grimmelshausen's 'anti-hero' echoes more the tradition of *Till Eulenspiegel* and related narratives than the Spanish picaresque. In England J. Fitzmaurice Kelly, in appraising Mabbe's presence in his own translation of the *Guzmán*, states that 'there may creep into it a reflexion or an amplification, but by his tastes and his generation he had no temptation to prune' (p. xxxiii). One of the earliest non-Spanish references to the *Lazarillo* indicates 'that it was regarded as a peculiarly Spanish product. To Englishmen of the sixteenth and seventeenth centuries..., *Lazarillo de Tormes* and its national successors were proof from the Devil's own mouth of his chosen people's hypocrisy, idolatry, and barbarism' (Kearful, p. 377). As works of fiction they were adapted enthusiastically from Spanish originals as well as from French translations. It may be that, because England had the strongest 'native' traditions of criminal biographies, anatomies of roguery and beggar books in Europe, Spanish narratives remained distinctly 'Spanish'. Many of the picaresque conventions were passed on through Smollett's translation of *Gil Blas*, an anti-picaresque narrative based on a long history of French adaptations and translations.

After the eighteenth century in Europe it is no longer possible to speak of picaresque novels, and even, as Claudio Guillén has stated, of a 'picaresque theme' (p. 100). In France for instance, the convention of the first-person narrative had already become firmly linked with the so-called 'memoir-novel'. Lesage's use of it in

Gil Blas was in many ways as 'anachronistic' as the novel's Spanish setting. And in England to call *Tom Jones* a picaresque novel is to ignore completely the fact that *Don Quixote*, not *Guzmán* and his followers, was Fielding's model. Fielding's *The Life of Mr Jonathan Wild the Great* (1743), while similar in some ways to the Spanish picaresque, is in reality 'more closely related to the Marlovian hero, possibly through such intermediaries as Don Tomaso, than to Lazarillo de Tormes ... As literary parody he derives from the criminal biographies which were simply about the rogue just hanged and all those exemplary biographies that reached a climax for Fielding in Cibber's *Apology*' (Paulson, pp. 73–4). Many works of Captain Frederick Marryat (1792–1848), Godwin's *The Adventures of Caleb Williams* (1794), Bulwer Lytton's *Paul Clifford* (1830) and Thackeray's *Barry Lyndon* (1844) descend from the English tradition of Defoe, Fielding and Smollett.

Several novels of Charles Dickens (1812–1870) have been called picaresque mainly because of their so-called 'realistic' portrayal of a 'hostile' society through which an 'individual' makes his way. Perhaps Dickens understood the picaresque tradition in just such a loose sense. In the preface to *Pickwick Papers* his intention was to 'place before the reader a constant succession of characters and incidents'. We have seen already that this episodic structure is a convention of many modes of fiction and not just of the picaresque. J. Hillis Miller, however, calls the novel 'Victorian picaresque', but it may be more accurate to say that Dickens is working within an 'anti-picaresque myth'. Pickwick is in no sense a *pícaro*. Dickens' second novel, *Oliver Twist* (1838), concentrates on the adventures of a single hero from his birth, who, according to S. Eoff, 'brings to mind the picaro in the role of a homeless and friendless child who finds himself at the mercy of an unsympathetic society' (p. 440). But Dickens tells us in essence that *Oliver Twist* is anti-picaresque: 'I wished to show, in little Oliver, the principle of Good surviving through every adverse circumstance, and triumphing at last'. Oliver will not end up a failure. The collective problem for all the characters in *Oliver Twist* is not 'how to "succeed", how to "rise in the world", but how to live in this world at all ... Neither the social world nor the world of nature is willing to give them the means of life. The thieves would have starved to death

either in or out of a workhouse if they had not turned to crime...'
(Miller, p. 37). While Oliver is not a *pícaro* in the strict sense,
Fagin definitely reveals some of the traits of the classical type. He is
reminiscent of Ginés de Pasamonte or of some of the thieves in
Monipodio's den in Seville. Fagin, of course, ends up on the
gallows, whereas Oliver chooses to go with Mr Brownlow, a symbol
of good. Oliver certainly has accomplished more than mere survival;
he has become the adopted son of Mr Brownlow, an event which
points to his acceptance by society and to his acquisition of freedom
in a 'happy' world.

By the end of the eighteenth and nineteenth centuries, the
pícaro had become almost exclusively a satirist or had been replaced
by the anti-*pícaro*. In seventeenth-century Spain, as we have seen,
the picaresque genre had prepared the groundwork for an 'anti-
genre' in which repentance, virtue, stability and 'success' triumphed
at the end of a life of roguery. The basic idea that a virtuous
man could work himself out of the most adverse circumstances,
primarily poverty, to ultimate prosperity and honour finds its
definitive form in America in the popular fiction of Horatio Alger,
Jr (1834–1899). The 'myth' of the classical picaresque, however, is
not forgotten. Its purest twentieth-century mutations seem to exist
in novels such as Ralph Ellison's *The Invisible Man* (1952), Saul
Bellow's *The Adventures of Augie March, A Novel* (1953), Thomas
Mann's *Bekenntnisse des Hochstaplers Felix Krull: Der Memoiren
erster Teil* (*Confessions of Felix Krull; Confidence Man*) (1954) and
J. P. Donleavy's *The Ginger Man* (1955).

4

Epilogue: pícaros *in the Promised Land*

Into Seville streamed the hungry crowd of emigrants to America,
impoverished gentlemen hoping to restore their family fortunes, soldiers seeking adventure, young men of no property
hoping to make good, and along with them the dregs of Spanish
society, branded thieves, bandits, tramps all hoping to find some
lucrative activity overseas, debtors fleeing pressing creditors and
husbands fleeing nagging wives. To all of them, the Indies
represented the promised land ... (Fernand Braudel, II, 740)

Our efforts to retrace the itinerary of a type of narrative fiction
have guided us across national as well as literary boundaries. At the
end of the *Buscón* Pablos sailed to the New World to look for a
better life and returned to Spain, having found life in the Indies
worse. Defoe, on the other hand, directed Moll Flanders across the
Atlantic Ocean where she found prosperity and honour. Quevedo
insisted on his protagonist's status as a 'failed outsider' (the phrase
is Guillén's) to the end; Defoe returned his protagonist to
England to live a life of leisure. Pablos is imprisoned within a
closed circle. He is another Sisiphus whose career is summed up
by Guzmán's words: 'And being come now to the height of all my
labors and paines-taking, and when I was to have received the
reward of them, and to take mine ease after all this toyle, the stone
rolled down, and I was forced like Sisiphus, to beginne the world
anew, and to fall afresh to my work' (Mabbe, IV, 220). Moll's
success breaks the circle of poverty and failure by redefining the
nature of criminality itself. Pablos, however, discovers that the
Promised Land offers only promises.

The *pícaro* can also be viewed as the 'anti-hero' with a 'thousand'
faces. His protean nature is implicit in his changing masks and

landscapes according to Ulrich Wicks: 'The picaro is a protean figure who can not only serve many masters but play different roles, and his essential characteristic is his inconstancy – of life roles, of self-identity – his own personality flux in the face of an inconstant world. Paradoxically, nothing is more constant than inconstancy itself' (p. 245). Edmond Cros' and Everett Hesse's descriptions of Guzmán and Pablos as protean figures preview Wicks' observations and seem to elevate the *pícaro*'s wanderings and adventures to the level of a myth, to a story or plot, in Guillén's words, 'that is "already alive", and has been so for many centuries' (p. 99). When we speak of myth Guillén suggests that we refer to two things:

> to myth as a precipitate of cultural history, as that special recognition of the *déjà vu* that alludes not so much to considerations of genre or technique as to a simple narrative or dramatic theme, plot, or story, and to the pleasure one derives from reading or seeing it once more; and secondly, to the fact that this pleasure implies a reader who remembers and is 'in the know'. A literary myth (though not in the occult sense) assumes a certain cultural continuity and the participation of the reader in this continuity. (Guillén, p. 99)

While these meditations on the picaresque myth help to explain its psychological appeal for readers throughout the centuries, they also reflect the individual author's stance within his own society, or, as Guillén puts it, 'the living man's understanding of himself' (*ibid.*). Quevedo determined that Pablos would not rise above the social level of a thief and *converso*. As a satirist he was protecting what he saw as fundamental values of seventeenth-century Spanish society, which, he insists in many of his works, had already degenerated to a lamentable state. Defoe on the contrary conceived the fictive possibility of breaking through class barriers by making life into a successful mercantile experience. Quevedo was an 'insider' protecting his position against would-be 'gentlemen' like Pablos and more subtly, against crypto-'noblemen' like Pablos' boyhood friend, Don Diego. Defoe was an 'outsider' who did not meet with the same prosperity as his protagonists. In this sense, then, the convenventional upward struggle represented the confrontation between two myths: the 'myth' of the failed outsider and the 'myth' of a society or world which defined him as such.

In the seventeenth century the New World symbolized an escape from the hierarchical society of Spain. Seville was populated with *indianos*, Spaniards who had returned home after making their fortunes in America. This was the myth that Pablos sought to share. In the eighteenth century the English colonies fulfilled the same function. *Moll Flanders* reveals how even a transported criminal can 'earn' his freedom from poverty through careful investment. In the nineteenth century popular myth defined the United States as a Promised Land with unparalleled opportunities for getting ahead. The numerous novels of Horatio Alger, Jr, which sold over 30,000,000 copies, extolled the virtues of clean living and hard work and promised wealth and success to boys who were willing to follow the example of characters like 'Ragged Dick' and 'Tattered Tom'. As Hugh Kenner recently phrased it: 'The Alger plot was simple and oft repeated. One started meagerly; one shined shoes or sold papers and saved one's earnings; and one got on' (p. 21). The 'American way', starting at the bottom, echoes the starting point of the *pícaro*. One of Alger's most popular novels, *Struggling Upward; or, Luke Larkin's Luck* (ed. Crouse, N.Y., 1945) epitomizes this myth of freedom and opportunity. Luke was:

> the son of a carpenter's widow, living on narrow means, and so compelled to exercise the strictest economy. Luke worked where he could, helping the farmers in hay-time and ready to do odd jobs for any one in the village who desired his services. He filled the position of janitor at the school which he attended, sweeping out twice a week and making the fires. He had a pleasant expression, and a bright, resolute look, a warm heart, and a clear intellect, and was probably, in spite of his poverty, the most popular boy in Groveton. (pp. 3–4)

After leaving home, Luke remains true to his virtuous upbringing and, getting a 'lucky break', returns to Groveton to become part of the staff at the local bank. The distilled Alger 'story' is the essence of the 'anti-picaresque' myth in its fully evolved state. And even though many of the experiences of the 'anti-*pícaro*' are similar in nature to the misfortunes and defeats of the *pícaro*, the outcome is quite distinct.

A curious recent mutation of this Alger anti-picaresque myth is an authentic autobiography, Claude Brown's *Manchild in the Promised Land* (N.Y., 1965). Brown as a 'character' in his book is far from being a virtuous person in the conventional sense, but by participating in gang-wars, theft and narcotics trafficking, he adheres to the norms of life in Harlem. However, when he attends college and becomes a law student at one of America's leading universities, his success turns him into an 'outsider' within his own community. Brown conceives his autobiography within the myth of America as a Promised Land. What he discovers and communicates to his readers is that, for blacks who abandon their traditional homes in the South and seek a better life in America's northern cities, the Promised Land is one vast slum, and the mythic Promise a monumental lie which enslaves and destroys his people. Brown's powerful 'black' displacement of the Alger myth is used as the weapon to destroy the very essence of the Algerian combination of hard work and luck. His ultimate and lasting 'success', however, is not so different from Lazarillo's: the writing of their *vidas* has produced both honour and fame.

The twentieth century has witnessed self-conscious imitations of the early picaresque, the *liber vagatorum* and criminal biography traditions. George Orwell's *Down and Out in London and Paris* (1933; rpt. N.Y., 1961), even though narrated from a first-person viewpoint, falls into the category of the beggar book. Aside from some echoes of the types of characters and adventures found in the *pícaro*'s life, *Down and Out* is primarily a book about poverty, a chronicle of society's lowest substrata, kitchen-boys, beggars and tramps. None of them is really a criminal; they are forced by infirmity or accident into a life they did not choose. The narrator, presumably 'Orwell', is among them by choice, a kind of rogue-journalist, functioning as an amateur sociologist. His stated purpose is to write 'a fairly trivial story, but I can only hope that it has been interesting in the same way as a travel diary is interesting' (p. 213). His real purpose, of course, is far more subtle and serious. The narrator shows the wastefulness and stupidity of a system which condemns men to the useless expending of energy. In this 1933 account one sees a strong indication of that social consciousness which in its maturity produced the highly satirical *Animal Farm* (1944) and *Nineteen-Eighty Four* (1949).

During these same years Jean Genet's career as a professional thief and beggar appeared in print as *Journal du Voleur* (1949; trans. B. Frechtman, N.Y., 1973). He records his experiences in 'real' Spain which he also defines as that 'region of myself which I have called Spain' (p. 268). Genet's diary is not a picaresque novel or even a criminal biography. His basic subjects are 'betrayal, theft and homosexuality' (p. 171). His status as an 'outsider', however, is clearly established:

> Abandoned by my family, I already felt it was natural to aggravate this condition by a preference for boys, and this preference by theft, and theft by crime or a complacent attitude in regard to crime. I thus resolutely rejected a world which had rejected me. (pp. 86–7)

Despite the fact that Genet's journal of thievery and beggary is written in the first-person style, it is only an episode in a 'life' that is always in the process of becoming. Within the traditions we have discussed, *The Thief's Journal* pertains to the *liber vagatorum* and criminal biographical strains, shared only to a degree by the picaresque. Genet is a sign of the authentically 'existential' man who comes to grips in writing with what he has made of himself. In this sense he echoes Lazarillo's struggle with language. Orwell observes without becoming part of his observations. His fiction is antiseptic compared to Genet's self-portrayal. Genet, in essence, *is* what he writes because he can be part of nothing else.

Like *Manchild in the Promised Land* both these books are presented to the reader as 'actual' experiences of their authors. However, the literary tradition of picaresque 'fiction' co-existed with works of this kind during the same years. Thomas Mann's *Confessions of Felix Krull* (trans. D. Lindley, N.Y., 1955) is cast into the literary form of the picaresque. Erich Heller writes that 'one of Felix Krull's literary ancestors is undoubtedly Mateo Alemán's *Guzmán de Alfarache, Pícaro*...' (p. 541). Among other possible 'sources', Heller adds, is *Simplicissimus*. Moreover, Mann's *Voyage with Don Quixote*, a journal he maintained while crossing the Atlantic in 1934, consists of his meditations on Cervantes' anti-romance. He would have come across Cervantes' criminal-author, Ginés de Pasamonte, whose 'life' was written in the pattern of the *Lazarillo* and the *Guzmán*.

Mann handles several picaresque conventions. The first-person viewpoint, in the manner of Lázaro, Guzmán and Pablos, functions to narrate the life of Felix as a character and to allow him to comment on his experiences through his direct addresses to the reader. Moreover, Krull is a self-conscious actor, exulting in his ability to be someone other than himself: 'My secret wealth – or this is how my dream-acquired riches seemed to me – transformed my uniform and my job into a role, a simple extension of my talent for "dressing up" ' (pp. 186–7). He discovers early that 'respectable' society rejects those who are or who look poor. Poverty prevents one from making a proper appearance. And like Lázaro, Guzmán and Pablos, he perceives that clothing can sometimes reverse the servant-master relationship: 'With a change of clothes and make-up, the servitors might often just as well have been the masters, and many of those who lounged in the deep wicker chairs, smoking their cigarettes, might have played the waiter. It was pure accident that the reverse was the fact, an accident of wealth; for an aristocracy of money is an accidental and interchangeable aristocracy' (p. 224). Mann arranges to have Felix 'become' his own father, as it were, a picaresque convention which appears both in the *Lazarillo* and the *Buscón*.

While all these elements echo the picaresque careers of previous servants, Felix's respect for women and marriage, hard work at the hotel, and the chain of accidents which bring good luck not bad, are reflections more of the anti-picaresque Algerian ideas than those of the down-and-out *pícaro*. Felix is, however, a 'confidence man', so much so that at times he deludes himself. He actually considers himself a gentleman, even in rags and working at menial tasks. We are allowed to see through the delusion that Mann has created for Krull, but Krull himself, unconscious of the discrepancies, seems to have been taken in by the *real* trickster, Thomas Mann. If so, the motif of the 'trickster-tricked', one of the featured conventions of the genre from the *Lazarillo* onward, has been elevated in *Felix Krull* to express the relationship between the author and his narrator.

The mythic figure which stands behind Felix, and perhaps Mann the 'author', is repeatedly mentioned throughout the novel. He is Hermes and, according to R. Heilman, 'comes into the Krull story as the patron deity of Felix as thief..., identified with luck, travel, theft and trickery, priapism, eloquence, and the arts – over all of which Hermes presided' (p. 559). This leads Heilman to conclude that Mann 'was clearly infusing into the picaresque something of the mythic that absorbed him' (*ibid.*) in his 'creation' of a picaresque myth. We have already seen that Sisyphus and Proteus were invoked as mythic counterparts of the *pícaro*. All three represent fundamental aspects of the *pícaro* and of his relationship to society: the unceasing repetition of hardship and failure, the changing masks and careers and now the trickster-thief. Not only do these mythic figures apply to the *pícaro* as a character; they also characterize his status as author and as artist. But the idea of the *pícaro* as artist was not an invention of Mann. Lázaro clearly saw himself in this role, and Cervantes emphasized the author-*pícaro* in his creation of Ginés de Pasamonte. If Cervantes was one of the first to recognize the *pícaro* as an 'artist' who manipulated fiction as well as life, Mann inherited the concept and transformed him into a twentieth-century 'con-man'.

The picaresque in Europe does not end with *Felix Krull*. Gunter Grass's *Die Blechtrommel* (*The Tin Drum*) (1959) is the biography of Oskar who exhibits the same 'equivocal dissatisfaction with the real' (Guillén, p. 103). And in Spain, Camilo José Cela explicitly recalls the early tradition in his *Nuevas andanzas y desventuras de Lazarillo de Tormes* (*New Travels and Misfortunes of Lazarillo de Tormes*) (1946). His earlier novel, *La familia de Pascual Duarte* (1942) features the same violence, black humour, grotesqueness and narrative technique of Quevedo's *Buscón*. The production of novels written in the picaresque tradition seems to have burgeoned during the peculiarly uneasy 'peace' which followed the Spanish Civil War and World War II. Consequently their narrations share the tonality of earlier 'war' fictions such as *Estebanillo González* and *Simplicissimus*. But it was in the United States, to return to the geography at the beginning of this section, where the picaresque has found its strongest and most authentic voices.

The myth of the failed outsider can be found in the novels of Ralph Ellison, J. P. Donleavy and Saul Bellow. The principal action of Bellow's *Adventures of Augie March* (N.Y., 1953) occurs in the period from the beginning of the Great Depression in the late 1920s to the end of the second world war, two historical events which have had a monumental impact on the fabric of American society. Augie's life follows a conventional episodic pattern, but it is the quality of these episodes which places his story within the picaresque myth of the failed outsider.

The question of Augie's parentage is never resolved. His father abandoned the family when Augie was small and two references (pp. 227, 538) suggest that Augie is never sure of his legitimacy. In his relations with society, he exhibits many of the characteristics we have come to associate with the *pícaro*. He is the product of an urban environment who falls naturally into a pattern of delinquency, stealing 'coal off coal cars, clothes from the lines, rubber balls from the dime store . . .' (p. 17), later supporting himself as a thief, and finally, as a much more sophisticated black marketeer in Paris. Indifferent to society's traditional standards of morality, he does not see himself as a real criminal but only as a person 'on the wrong side of the universal wide line with the worse or weaker part of humankind . . .' (p. 53). Augie does not aspire to become a gentleman; he does not aspire at all, hoping instead that 'somebody would die and leave me everything' (p. 508). Like Pablos of the *Buscón*, Augie stubbornly pursues what he calls a 'higher independent fate' (p. 482), refusing to accept a predetermined fate. He may at times wish to quit his 'pilgrimage' (p. 482) but in the end he can 'laugh at nature – including eternity – that it thinks it can win over us and the power of hope' (p. 607). The 'internal' Augie is a shadow of Sisyphus, more of Camus than of Greece, who finds himself caught in the absurdity of repetition and failure but who at the same time regains his strength through laughter.

J. P. Donleavy's *The Ginger Man* is the story of Sebastian Dangerfield, a twenty-seven-year-old American, who considers himself a law student but who manages rarely to attend a lecture or look inside a book at Trinity College. He drinks his way through successive episodes in Dublin and London while waiting to become rich either by miracle or by accident – more specifically – by the death of his father. *The Ginger Man* contains many of the conventions we have associated with the picaresque. Dangerfield is obsessive about food, but his elegant tastes put the Spanish *pícaro* to shame. However, the ruses he invents when in quest of an especially succulent roast or a plump chicken echo the Machiavellian plots of the Spanish *pícaros* in search of 'bread and cheese'. His concern with his 'image', especially with his proper British accent, reflects a self-acknowledged role as an actor. But despite his seeming gregariousness, he is alone in the world. He is also 'alone' within himself, without any idea where he has come from nor where he is going in life: 'I'm alone. And took the train. The land was gray. And when I got here all the others were taking big cars and taxis everywhere and I had no one and just walked down the platform wondering what to do' (pp. 294–5).

Donleavy's novel, even though centrally concerned with the 'failed outsider', lacks many of the conventions which would place it firmly in the picaresque tradition. It is not an autobiography beginning with the birth of the hero. The narrative is not even strictly first person. It shifts constantly between the first- and third-person voices, emblematic perhaps of the underlying divided 'self' of its hero. Dangerfield is an outsider not because he is a poor man attempting to get by in a hostile society but because of the nature of his 'personality'. It is he who is hostile, not society. His poverty is not of the conventional sort either. It is the middle-class 'poverty' of the twentieth century. He feels himself poor because he is not extremely rich. He wants above all else to be a gentleman, a wealthy gentleman.

Dangerfield lives (and loves) by his wits in an urban landscape, under the constant threat of violence, his episodic adventures punctuated by scrapes with the police, the landlord and his creditors. His relationships with women are transitory because he views them as little more than temporary servants who fulfil his needs in the kitchen and bedroom. He can neither fulfil nor relinquish his fantasies; his expectations are in perpetual conflict with the reality of his situation. In sum Dangerfield is an imbalanced hero, carried along by the doubling and oscillating fantasies of his life which constitute his status as an outsider even to himself.

Ralph Ellison's *Invisible Man* (N.Y., 1952) features a narrating hero who is so 'outside' that he is 'invisible'. Ellison's narrator is a black man in the United States. The fact that he is nameless contributes to his invisibility. Being invisible means that 'people refuse to see me' (p. 3). But it also means being out of rhythm with things:

> Invisibility, let me explain, gives one a slightly different sense of time, you're never quite on the beat. Sometimes you're ahead and sometimes behind. Instead of the swift and imperceptible flowing of time, you are aware of its nodes, those points where time stands still or from which it leaps ahead. And you slip into the breaks and look around. (p. 7)

The trajectory of his goals early in life point upward, but the reality of his experiences points in a different direction. His ultimate acknowledgement that he is 'invisible' allows him to make a 'success' out of travelling downward. It is appropriate, then, that his final home in the novel is a 'hole in the ground' under the streets of New York, a 'warm hole' (p. 5), a kind of concrete and asphalt uterus where he has hibernated while developing a sense of his form through the writing of his 'life'. This uterine refuge will give birth to his 'disembodied voice' (p. 439), still invisible because it is only a voice:

> And, as I said before, a decision has been made. I'm shaking off the old skin and I'll leave it here in the hole. I'm coming out, no less invisible without it, but coming out nevertheless. (pp. 438–9)

What has led to his refuge in a subterranean world and to his final decision to abandon it? The invisible man's career is a series of rejections which begins soon after he graduates from high school. He receives a scholarship to attend a prominent black college, but in attempting to ingratiate himself with a white trustee, he unwittingly angers the college president. As a result he is dismissed from school and sent to New York, his pockets stuffed with what he believes to be letters of recommendation for a summer job. He discovers, however, that they inform various 'friends' of the college that under no circumstances will he be allowed to return. He does manage to find a job in a paint factory in New York but ends up in the factory hospital because of an accident. Recovering from his brief experience as a paint mixer, he becomes involved with a black 'brotherhood' movement in Harlem and believes he has found his place in life. But he is betrayed by his new 'friends' who have used him to advance themselves. Attempting to reconcile black and white communities in Harlem, he finds only frustration and rejection and is forced into a cold, objective reappraisal of his life:

> And now all past humiliations became precious parts of my experience, and for the first time, leaning against that stone wall in the sweltering night, I began to accept my past and, as I accepted it, I felt memories welling up within me. It was as though I'd learned suddenly to look around corners; images of past humiliations flickered through my head and I saw that they were more than separate experiences. They were me; they defined me. I was my experiences and my experiences were me ... (p. 383)

Invisible Man is picaresque because it is the autobiography of a failed and rejected outsider. But his failure is a qualified one in that at the end of the novel he is no longer estranged from himself. He has made his way up the ladder of the brotherhood through his witty tongue and his ability to move the poor of Harlem to action through words, the same words he uses to write his 'life'. Though not a trickster in the traditional sense, he deceives himself into thinking that the value of his life is determined by the values of the community around him. Role-playing, a central motif in the protean career of the *pícaro*, is present throughout the novel. But it becomes doubly self-conscious when the narrator buys a pair of dark glasses and a hat to assure his safe passage through Harlem streets. Even old friends fail to recognize him. But masks, he discovers, facilitate his invisibility in a society which seems to demand that the face behind the mask become the mask itself. He rejects this mode of existence because it denies the fundamental importance of an individualizing past.

The convention of the first-person narrative fulfils the same function that it had in the *Lazarillo* and the *Guzmán*. Like Lázaro, the invisible man writes his life to account for his 'final' present situation. His downward movement in society is seriously viewed as a 'success' because it has enabled him to come to some permanent understanding of himself. While Lázaro literally becomes a 'voice' in the community as the town crier, the invisible man's disembodied voice takes form through the writing of his book. And like Guzmán, he punctuates his narrative with interior monologues which stand contrapuntally to the adventures he recounts. If the *Guzmán* is the story of a 'soul', then *Invisible Man* is the story of an 'invisibility' (loss or absence of soul) out of which emerges an awareness of individual value. Ellison takes picaresque conventions to their fullest and most profound development by revitalizing their original functions. The *pícaro*'s 'tainted' ancestry defines him as an outsider in the same manner that a black man's colour determines his position in twentieth-century America. The picaresque novel finally becomes what it pretended to be all along: the autobiography of a 'nobody' and his adventures in a 'repressive' society. The discovery of the picaresque as a mode of fiction is a failing enterprise in itself; the *pícaro*'s self-creation in words is at odds with his attempt to be more than 'mere' language. The very nature of his 'speaking' presence is obliterated through the 'writing' of his life.

Bibliography

The following bibliography on the picaresque is extremely selective. I have included studies from which I have quoted in the text as well as many articles and books I never mention. All have contributed substantially toward my approach to the picaresque. My greatest debts, too infrequently acknowledged, are to F. W. Chandler, C. Guillén, A. A. Parker and F. Rico. Each chapter has its own bibliographical listing in alphabetical order. In the rare cases in which I have referred to a study cited in another chapter, I ask for the reader's patience while he finds the first reference. Finally, the most up-to-date and complete bibliography on the picaresque is J. Laurenti's *Bibliografía de la literatura picaresca*, Metuchen, N.J., 1973.

1: PROLOGUE

Allen, W., *The English Novel: A Short Critical History*, New York, 1954.

Alter, R., *Rogue's Progress: Studies in the Picaresque Novel*, Cambridge, Mass., 1964.

Chandler, F. W., *Romances of Roguery: An Episode in the History of the Novel. Part I: The Picaresque Novel in Spain*, New York, 1899.

Chandler, F. W., *The Literature of Roguery*, 2 vols, London, Boston, New York, 1907.

Frohock, W. M., 'The Idea of the Picaresque', *Yearbook of Comparative and General Literature*, 16 (1967), 43–52.

Guillén, C., *Literature as System: Essays Toward the Theory of Literary History*, Princeton, 1971.

De Haan, F., *An Outline of the History of the Novela Picaresca in Spain*, The Hague, New York, 1903.

Hassan, I., *Radical Innocence: The Contemporary American Novel*, Princeton, 1961.

Miller, S., *The Picaresque Novel*, Cleveland, 1967.

Parker, A. A., *Literature and the Delinquent: The Picaresque Novel in Spain and Europe 1599–1753*, Edinburgh, 1967.

Paulson, R., *The Fictions of Satire*, Baltimore, 1967.

Whitbourn, C., ed., *Knaves and Swindlers: Essays on the Picaresque Novel in Europe*, London, 1974.

Wicks, U., 'Picaro, Picaresque: The Picaresque in Literary Scholarship', *Genre*, 5 (1972), 153–216.

2: SPAIN

Alemán, M., *Guzmán de Alfarache*, ed. F. Rico, Barcelona, 1967.

Alemán, M., *The Rogue or the Life of Guzman de Alfarache*, trans. J. Mabbe, with an introduction by J. Fitzmaurice-Kelly, 4 vols, New York (rpt), 1967.

Bataillon, M., *Pícaros y picaresca: 'La pícara Justina'*, Madrid, 1969.

Braudel, F., *The Mediterranean and the Mediterranean World in the Age of Philip II*, trans. from the French by Sian Reynolds, 2 vols, New York, 1972.

Corominas, J., *Diccionario crítico etimológico de la lengua castellana*, 4 vols, Bern, 1956.

Covarrubias, S. de, *Tesoro de la lengua castellana o española*, Madrid, 1611, ed. M. de Riquer, Barcelona, 1943.

Ettinghausen, H., *Francisco de Quevedo and the Neostoic Movement*, Oxford, 1972.

González, G., *El guitón Honofre*, ed. H. G. Carrasco, Chapel Hill, N. C., 1973.

González-Ollé, F., ' "Guerras civiles de Flandes", poema épico inédito', *Boletín de la Real Academia Española*, 45 (1965), 141–84.

González-Ollé, F., 'Nuevos testimonios tempranos de "pícaro" y palabras afines', *Ibero-Romania*, 1 (1969), 56–8.

Haley, G., *Vicente Espinel and 'Marcos de Obregón': A Life and its Literary Representation*, Providence, 1959.

Jones, R. O., *A Literary History of Spain. The Golden Age: Prose and Poetry. The Sixteenth and Seventeenth Centuries*, London, 1971.

La vida de Lazarillo de Tormes y de sus fortunas y adversidades, ed. F. Rico, Barcelona, 1967.

The Life of Lazarillo of Tormes: His Fortunes and Misfortunes, trans. R. S. Rudder, New York, 1973.

Lázaro Carreter, F., '*Lazarillo de Tormes' en la picaresca*, Barcelona, 1972.

Molho, M., ed., *Romans picaresques espagnols*, Paris, 1968.

Morris, C. B., *The Unity and Structure of Quevedo's 'Buscón'*, Hull, 1965.

Parker, A. A., 'The Psychology of the *picaro* in *El Buscón*', *Modern Language Review*, 42 (1947), 58–69.

Parker, G., *The Army of Flanders and the Spanish Road 1567–1659: The Logistics of Spanish Victory and Defeat in the Low Countries' War*, Cambridge, 1972.

Paulson, R., *Satire and the Novel in Eighteenth-Century England*, New Haven, 1967.

Quevedo, F. de., *The Swindler*, trans. M. Alpert, Harmondsworth, 1969.

Rico, F., *La novela picaresca y el punto de vista*, Barcelona, 1970.

Samaha, J., *Law and Order in Historical Perspective: The Case of Elizabethan Essex*, New York, 1974.

3: EUROPE

Adam, A., *Histoire de la littérature française au XVIIe siècle: L'époque d'Henri IV et de Louis XIII*, 5 vols, 1948–65; I, Paris, 1948.

Bahner, W., 'Quelques observations sur le genre picaresque', *Roman et lumières au XVIIIe siècle*, Paris, 1970, pp. 64–72.

Bowers, F., 'Thomas Nashe and the Picaresque Novel', *Humanistic Studies in Honor of John Calvin Metcalf*, Charlottesville, 1941, pp. 12–27.

Brun, F., *Littérature et société*, Brussels, 1967.

Crimes et criminalité en France sus l'Ancien Régime, 17–18 siècles, in *Cahiers des Annales*, 33, Paris, 1971.

Defoe, D., *The Compleat English Gentleman*, ed. K. D. Bülbring, London, 1890.

Defoe, D., *The Fortunes and Misfortunes of The Famous Moll Flanders*, ed. M. Schorer, The Modern Library, New York, 1950.

Eoff, S., '*Oliver Twist* and the Spanish Picaresque Novel', *Studies in Philology*, 54 (1957), 440–7.

Fritz, E., 'Grimmelshausens *Simplicissimus* und seine spanischen Verwandten', *Merkur*, 66 (1953), 753–64.

Frohock, W. M., 'The "Picaresque" in France before *Gil Blas*', *Yale French Studies*, 38 (1967), 222–9.

Grimmelshausen, H. J. von, *Simplicius Simplicissimus*, trans. G. Schulz-Behrend, New York, 1965.

Kearful, F. J., 'Spanish Rogues and English Foundlings: On the Disintegration of Picaresque', *Genre*, 4 (1970), 376–91.

Lesage, A. R., *The Adventures of Gil Blas of Santillane*, trans. T. Smollett; ed. G. Saintsbury, 3 vols, London, 1881.

Miller, J. H., *Charles Dickens: The World of His Novels*, Cambridge, Mass., 1968.

Novak, M., 'Freedom, Libertinism, and the Picaresque', in *Studies in Eighteenth-Century Culture*, 3 ('Racism in the Eighteenth Century'), Cleveland, 1973.

Randall, D. B. J., *The Golden Tapestry: A critical Survey of Non-Chivalric Spanish Fiction in English Translation, 1543–1657*, Durham, N. C., 1963.

Reynier, G., *Le Roman réaliste au XVIIe siècle*, Paris, 1914.

Richetti, J., *Popular Fiction before Richardson: Narrative Patterns 1700–1739*, Oxford, 1969.

Rotzer, H. G., *Picaro – Landstortzer – Simplicius: Studien zum niederen Roman in Spanien und Deutschland*, Darmstadt, 1972.

Sims, E. R., 'An Italian Translation of *Lazarillo de Tormes*', *Hispanic Review*, 3 (1935), 331–7.

Smollett, T., *The Adventures of Count Fathom*, ed. George Saintsbury, 2 vols, London, 1928.

Smollet, T., *The Adventures of Roderick Random*, A Signet Classic, with an 'Afterward' by J. Barth, New York, 1964.

Thomas, H., 'The English Translations of Quevedo's *La vida del Buscón*', *Revue Hispanique*, 81 (1933), 282–99.

4: EPILOGUE

Brown, N. O., *Hermes the Thief: The Evolution of a Myth*, A Vintage Book, New York, 1969.

Cros, E., *Protèe et le Gueux: Recherches sur les origines et la nature du récit picaresque dans 'Guzman de Alfarache'*, Paris, 1967.

Frohock, W. M., 'The Failing Center: Recent Fiction and the Picaresque Tradition', *Novel*, 3 (1969), 62–9.

Heilman, R., 'Variations on Picaresque (*Felix Krull*)', *The Sewanee Review*, 66 (1958), 547–77.

Heller, E., 'Parody, Tragic and Comic: Mann's *Doctor Faustus* and *Felix Krull*', *The Sewanee Review*, 66 (1958), 519–46.

Hesse, E., 'The Protean Changes in Quevedo's *Buscón*', *Kentucky Romance Quarterly*, 16 (1969), 243–59.

Kenner, H., *A Homemade World*, New York, 1975.

Schleussner, B., *Der neopikareske Roman: Pikareske Elemente in der Strukter moderner Englischer Romane 1950–1960*, Bonn, 1969.

Wicks, U., 'The Nature of Picaresque Narrative', *Publications of the Modern Language Association*, 89 (1974), 240–9.

Index